THE DIVA
NEXT DOOR

*How to Be a Singing Star
Wherever You Are*

JILL SWITZER

D0818687

34 13219-4285

ALLWORTH PRESS
NEW YORK

To Lindsey, my heart

08 07 06 05   5 4 3 2 1

Published by Allworth Press
An imprint of Allworth Communications, Inc.
10 East 23rd Street, New York, NY 10010

Cover design by Derek Bacchus
Interior illustrations by Shannon Wunderlich
Interior design and composition by Sharp Des!gns, Lansing, MI
The epigraphs on pages 1, 6, 76, and 126 come from *Like a Butterfly* © 2002 Jill Switzer.

ISBN: 1-58115-410-0

LIBRARY OF CONGRESS CATALOGING-IN-PUBLICATION DATA
Switzer, Jill.
    The diva next door : how to be a singing star wherever you are / Jill Switzer.
        p. cm.
    Includes bibliographical references, videography, and index.
    1. Singing—Vocational guidance. 2. Women singers. I. Title.
    ML3795.S92 2005
    783.6'023—dc22
                                    2004028829

Printed in Canada

Contents

Acknowledgments vi

About the Author vii

***Introduction: I'm Every Woman: If I Can Do It,
You Can, Too*** 1
My "Aha" Moment • The Journey • Point A to Point Diva

PHASE 1

The Verse: Building a Solid Foundation

1 ***It Don't Mean a Thing If It Ain't Got That Swing:
Honoring Your Passion to Sing*** 9
You Know Your Passion Is Singing If . . . • Time Is Not the Enemy
• Define Your Goal • Diversity Is Key • Beware of Naysayers
• You Know What's Best for You • Just Rewards • The Diva
Readiness Exercise • A Good Start • To Sum It Up

2 ***Sing, Sing a Song: Getting (and Keeping) Your Voice
in Shape for the Stage*** 25
Vocal Hitches • Help Is on the Way • Practice • Further
Instruction • A Healthy Voice • Fending Off Colds • A Word
from Mark Widick, M.D. • To Sum It Up

3 ***I'm Coming Out: Venturing into Your Local Music Scene*** 43
Live Music Venues • The Video/DVD Store • Snack Time •
The Musical Instrument and Equipment Store • Online Music

Communities and Resources • The Library or Bookstore
• The Newsstand • School/College Campuses • Surrounding
Areas • The Karaoke Store • The Value of a Thank-You Note
• "Ongoing" Is the Key Word • What Your Choices Reveal
• To Sum It Up

4 *Let's Get Physical: Your Body Is Your Instrument* 59
Exercise • A Complete Fitness Program • Program Burnout
• "Diet" Is a Four-Letter Word • Mom Knew Best • Girls Just
Wanna Have Fun • The Wee Small Hours • Looking the Part
• To Sum It Up

PHASE 2

The Bridge: Making the Transition from Hobbyist to Professional

5 *Get Ready: Fine-Tuning Your Act* 79
Repertoire • Organize a Songbook • Bust a Move • Classic
Songs • Because Practical Matters • Stand Tall • To Sum It Up

6 *Ain't Nothing Like the Real Thing: You're On!* 93
Search High and Low • Stage Fright • Ooze Divaness • Etiquette
• It's All about Relationships • Self-Promotion • Mailing List
• Daily Practice • Growing Pains • Comfort Food • To Sum It Up

7 *A Woman's Worth: Investments in Your Future Success* 109
Music Purchases • Wardrobe • Polishers • A Diva Résumé
• Get the Word Out • To Sum It Up

PHASE 3

The Chorus: Hallelujah, the Diva Is Revealed!

8 *A Star Is Born: Shining at Your Audition* 129
The Process ● The Day Has Arrived ● Be Discerning
● Beware of Band Romance ● Business Sense ● Organization
● The Agent's Role ● Self-Sabotage ● To Sum It Up

9 *There's No Stopping Us Now: The Ins and Outs*
   of Highly Successful Gigging 145
Rehearsals ● Another Word (or Two) from Mark Widick, M.D.
● Gigs ● Natural and Home Remedies for a Hoarse Voice
● Setup and Breakdown ● Performing ● Special Gigs ● To Sum
It Up

10 *Born to Fly: Expanding Your Horizons* 165
Think of Each Gig as an Audition ● Continue Improving Your
Craft ● Take It to the Next Level ● To Sum It Up

Appendix A: Sample Thank-You Note 183
Appendix B: Sample Cover Letter/Bio 184
Appendix C: Sample Performance Agreement 185
Appendix D: Sample Wedding Reception
   Information Sheet 187

Recommended Books, Videos, and Web
   Sites for Divas 189

Diva Dictionary 193

Index 195

Acknowledgments

I would like to first thank my husband, Rich, for encouraging me in all of my creative endeavors with his patience, wisdom, musical genius, and amazing love. There are some special people who have been the wind at my back at one time or another on my diva journey, beginning with the Mills family, Marianne Flemming, Tony Lavender, John and Nicole Yarling, Rick and Robin Krive, and Dick and Frances Switzer—I am better for knowing all of you. Thanks also to Leticia Cisneros, the best student a teacher could ever learn from. Much gratitude to Cynthia MacGregor for being the great editor next door and to Kirk Friedland for his generous counsel. And much love to my brother and sister, Jeff and Pam, and my mother and father, Catherine and Jean Jenkins, for filling our home with glorious music.

About the Author

Jill Switzer is one of the most sought-after vocalists in South Florida. For the past fifteen years, she has performed at venues ranging from Donald Trump's Mar-A-Lago Club, to large outdoor amphitheaters, to Birdland in New York City. She and her husband's band, Heartbeat, held the much-coveted position of the house band at the Poinciana Club, a private club in Palm Beach whose members and guests included Tony Bennett, Steve and Eydie Gorme, Princess Stephanie of Monaco, and Wayne Newton. Jill has appeared on stage with Tony Award®–winner Faith Prince, Ann Hampton Callaway, and members of the Four Freshman. Her voice has been heard on a public radio concert broadcast, in commercial jingles across the United States, and most recently on the nationally syndicated weekly television show *Dick Robinson's Lifestyles and Music by the Sea*. She lives in Palm Beach, Florida.

I'm Every Woman

IF I CAN DO IT, YOU CAN, TOO

Sittin' on the front porch, watching the world go by,
Wonderin' to myself, what is the meaning of my life?
When there on my rocking chair a butterfly did light
And in that moment the answer was inspired. *

What woman hasn't, at least once, fantasized about being on stage in the spotlight, clad in something gorgeous that celebrates all her feminine glory, singing to an adoring audience? I know I always did. As a young girl, when I stood at the top of the stairs giving concerts to my two best friends (what a lovely audience), I knew without a doubt that I wanted to be a singing star. I didn't question my calling, even when my brother pleaded with my mom to make me stop singing all the time.

But sometime around high school, I started wondering if being a professional singer was a realistic goal. I mean, no snazzy-looking gal in an evening gown ever showed up on career day handing out pamphlets touting the great and many opportunities for vocalists in my area. I just couldn't envision how I could possibly make it in a business in which I had no formal education, and one that was,

* "Like a Butterfly" © 2002 Jill Switzer

according to all my sources, fickle, unstable, and dependent on managers, contacts, and lucky breaks in faraway big cities.

My "Aha" Moment

My doubts couldn't have been farther from the truth. My "aha" moment came six years later at a friend's wedding. I had just had a baby and was dreading the return to my nine-to-five, uninspiring job. I desperately wanted to find work that was fulfilling, exciting, and fun and that would allow me to spend more time with my newborn. And having just become a mother, I had begun to think more as a role model: I wondered how I was going to keep a straight face when the time came for me to pass on to my daughter that lustrous pearl of wisdom: "Follow your dreams." I certainly hadn't done that myself up to that point.

But a dream job that still allowed me to be the mother I wanted to be seemed like almost too much to ask—until that Sunday afternoon wedding. I had been told that the band entertaining at the reception was the best in town. My friend's parents had booked them months in advance and had paid top dollar. As I sat eating the chicken and enjoying the music, I suddenly had an epiphany. I focused on the female singer, and my destiny was revealed.

> The real power behind whatever success I have now was something I found within myself—something that's in all of us, I think—a little piece of God just waiting to be discovered.
>
> *Tina Turner*

I thought to myself, I can do that! I had always been in the school chorus, and I was even in a few garage bands in college, but I had never dared to dream that I could make a living as a professional vocalist—until that moment.

The Journey

The following Monday, I started calling entertainment agencies in the phone book asking if they knew of any bands that needed a singer. The stock answer was: "We're not in the business of putting bands together—we just book them." But finally, an agent in the *M*s happened to know of one wedding band whose female singer was moving out of state. They were in desperate need of a

> "I'm the lady next door when I'm not onstage.
> *Aretha Franklin*"

replacement. I auditioned the next day, learned twenty-five songs from their repertoire, and a week and a half later, I was singing at my first bona fide gig.

By way of a wacky, wonderful, "learn as you go" journey, I was eventually able to quit my day job to work as a professional vocalist, performing for royalty, the rich, and the famous, as well as singing commercial jingles and studio demos. I was thriving far from major music centers like Los Angeles, New York City, or Nashville, without the aid of a manager, a publicist, a stylist, a personal trainer, or even an assistant. And when the next-door neighbor yelled, "There goes 'the diva'!" as I was leaving for a gig one evening, I gladly took the title and ran with it.

Point A to Point Diva

In this book, I tell you everything you need to know to prosper as a singer in your local music market and beyond. I've already done the pavement pounding, door knocking, head-against-the-wall banging, and lesson-learning, so that you can take a direct route from point *A* to point Diva. I share the practical gems, the tricks of the trade, and the golden rules I've picked up so far, as well as tasty tidbits, diva quotes, and words of wisdom. But the most important thing I want you to learn from this book is this: Anyone—and, yes, that includes you—can be a diva without moving to a big city, breaking the bank,

> I totally do not believe in backup plans. If you want something that bad . . . go for it!
>
> *Kelly Clarkson*

or sacrificing your firstborn. So if you've always dreamed of being a sexy chanteuse but never knew how to make it à lucrative, local reality, let *The Diva Next Door: How to Be a Singing Star Wherever You Are* show you the way.

A DIVA NEXT DOOR SAYS . . .

I am a pharmacist by day, but on four weekend nights a month, I trade in the white lab coat for the black leather to sing in a classic rock band. Before I started performing, I was extremely frustrated because I had no creative outlet to balance the stressful concentration necessary in my profession. Now, I'm enjoying the best of both worlds—I can use my college education and live out my rock-and-roll fantasy. I love to see the reactions of co-workers or customers from the pharmacy out in the audience. They usually do a quick double take when they spot me up onstage, and then their jaws drop. — Leticia

The Verse

Building a Solid Foundation

The Verse

First thing that I'll do is change my earthbound ways.
From here on out the sky's the limit, it's a brand new day.
Show my brilliant colors singin', "This is who I am!"
Surrendering to heaven's perfect plan.

The verse is the first section of a song, and it serves to set up the tone and content of the rest of the song, just as the first phase of this book serves to set you up for a successful and rewarding career as a professional vocalist. I guide you through the mental, technical, and physical challenges that a diva-in-training will face. I share the most effective and cost-saving solutions to the problems that you are likely to run into, as well as inspirational stories and practices to keep you motivated and on track. I also give you several ideas on how to begin immersing yourself into your local music scene as first an observer and gatherer of knowledge.

There is no substitute for a solid foundation, so in order to avoid a major collapse down the road, it is crucial that you not skip any steps in this first phase. When you are truly ready to start singing in public, your careful study and preparation will be evident in your confidence level, singing ability, command of the stage, professionalism, and general music-business acumen. So let's get started!

CHAPTER 1

It Don't Mean a Thing If It Ain't Got That Swing

HONORING YOUR PASSION TO SING

Most of us are not child prodigies with a sparkling, undeniable talent that begs to be nurtured and fostered by parents and teachers. No, most of us have to search and experiment, or stumble upon that thing that makes us light up inside, that thing that is the magic ingredient to a fun life—

> I was a nothing kid. Not particularly good. Not particularly bad.
>
> *Dusty Springfield*

our passion. We may not, by society's standards anyway, even be very good at our passion, but it beckons us all the same. And if we ignore the call, we understand all too well that it don't mean a thing if it ain't got that swing.

By virtue of the fact that you were drawn to read this book, it is pretty safe to assume that singing is your passion, but I've included a list of symptoms just to be sure. If you can identify with two or more in the following list, you are definitely reading the right book, and we can get on with the business at hand.

You Know Your Passion Is Singing If . . .

✻ You sing everywhere, all the time.
✻ As a child, your play often involved singing.
✻ You've annoyed at least one friend or family member with your incessant singing.
✻ You are or were in your school chorus and/or church choir.
✻ You know the words to practically every song on the radio.
✻ You think karaoke is the most significant invention of the twentieth century.
✻ When you turn on the TV, you immediately flip to a music video channel.
✻ You have a ridiculously large music collection.
✻ You cry whenever you hear or see a great vocal performance.

Now that we've confirmed what your passion is, the next step is to commit to a course of action, to honor your calling. It is a precious and crucial time. Precious because you are bravely opening yourself up to judgment, from yourself and others, in order to learn and grow. And crucial because the door can slam shut in an instant of overwhelming insecurity, societal pressures, lack of focus, or negativity from those around you. The purpose of this chapter is to make sure that none of that happens, so listen up, girlfriend.

> " The biggest devil is me. I'm either my best friend or my worst enemy.
> *Whitney Houston* "

Time Is Not the Enemy

Please be kind to yourself and know that there are no time limitations or deadlines, and that the competition is always with yourself. I've divided the process of becoming a singing star into three phases, and it is irrelevant whether it takes you two weeks, two months, or two years to get through each phase. Singing well is a combination of desire, daily practice, and confidence, and the time it takes to achieve this meeting of the mind, body, and soul is as unique as the individual.

Late Bloomers

Since I, myself, am considered by some to be a "late bloomer," I know the pressures our youth-worshiping society can put on a gal. The message seems to be that if you don't have a record deal and a song at the top of the charts by the age of eighteen, you may as well hang up your microphone. And the talent seems to be getting younger every year. What's next—an infant pop star gurgling and cooing through a song on MTV? It's almost comical, except for the negative effect it has on many people, especially females. When I hear one of my thirteen-year-old voice students worrying that it's too late for her to choose singing as a career, I know that our obsession with youth has gone too far.

Older and Wiser

I'm here to tell you what I told her: The female voice only begins to reach its prime at the age of thirty. The real artistry for a vocalist comes when she can evoke powerful emotions in her audience when she sings, and I'm of the mind that most of us have to do a bit of living before this can happen. Every passing year is one more year of life experience that you can bring to a song. So think of your years as an advantage rather than a cross to bear, or worse, a big fat excuse not to pursue your dream.

> I'm in my prime. Dancers my age would be in their twilight
> by now, but for what I do, I've just arrived.
>
> *Renee Fleming*

One of the most moving and beautiful live performances I've ever been privileged enough to witness was the elegant, eighty-something Margaret Whiting singing her classic love song, "Come Rain or Come Shine." As she crooned about a love lasting through good times and bad, expressing a range of emotions from devotion to hope to sadness, I knew she knew exactly what she was singing about. The moment was stunning.

Define Your Goal

Take some time now to do some soul searching and start defining your ultimate goal. Be as specific as possible, and whatever you do, don't be afraid to dream too big or too small. What I mean by this is, try to disregard society's ideas of success and failure, and focus on what is truly your dream job. For instance, do you want to

> I followed my heart and figured
> that if I tried and failed, at least
> I'd know that I tried.
>
> *Michelle Branch*

supplement your income by staying local and singing only on the weekends? (Some people feel very strongly that by not relying solely on music to earn a living, the love they have for their craft remains untainted by money matters.) Do you have your heart set on quitting your day job and becoming a full-time professional vocalist? Or have you always pictured your name up in lights and yourself entertaining a stadium or concert hall full of enthusiastic fans? These questions are critical to explore so that you make choices along the way that support your ultimate goal.

Stay in Your Lane

When asked how to reach your ultimate goal, Tony Award®–winning Broadway baby, Faith Prince, can sum it up in four words: "Stay in your lane." Her dream when she arrived in New York City as a fresh-faced college grad (along with countless others) was to sing on Broadway. Rather than pack up and go home when auditions didn't immediately pan out, she packed up and for the next ten years appeared in just about every regional theater and summer stock across the country. Instead of giving up when her dream job didn't materialize, she decided to do what she loved anyway. She "stayed in her lane" and has been captivating audiences on Broadway, film, and television ever since.

> " The whirlwind of my recent successes was just a case of timing after years of hard work.
>
> *Jamie O'Neil* "

Making Choices

Let's say, for example, that your ultimate goal is to be the lead singer in an all-girl rock band. Even though there's no formula for making this happen, the "stay in your lane" mindset can guide you in making choices that are conducive to reaching your goal. Let's say that you have an evening free: You could (a) audition for the chorus of your community theater's production of *Tommy*, or you could (b) stay home and watch the latest episode of *Survivor* on TV. I've seen so many aspiring singers choose (b)—idly waiting for their dream job to suddenly present itself while ignoring terrific, albeit perhaps less ideal, opportunities to gain performing experience. They don't seem to understand that the big break they are waiting for will happen only if they are prepared when it presents itself. Now please excuse me as I proceed to belabor this point with a story, but it's that important.

Do the Work

In the past few years, I've had three students come to me for help in preparation for the *American Idol* auditions. I was thrilled to be involved because not only do I think these kinds of shows offer a great opportunity to undiscovered talent, but back in the day, I went a couple of rounds in the local *Star Search* competition, and I know what a valuable learning experience it can be. But my enthusiasm soon turned to frustration, because unfortunately all three students had one thing in common: They wanted the big payday without ever putting in a full day's work.

With only a short time to prepare, they missed lessons, didn't practice, and made excuses—and not one accepted an open invitation to sit in at my gig to work on performing her audition song in front of a live audience. I feel Simon's pain whenever I watch *American Idol*. It seems as if many of the contestants, much like my three former students, woke up one morning and suddenly decided to become pop stars. Conversely, all of the winners on the show have had long histories of performing in their schools, churches, or communities—in other words, they did the work.

Take Baby Steps

If you're like most women I know, you're already busy juggling school or a job or a family with any number of other obligations and commitments. The way to accomplish your ultimate goal in the midst of all the chaos is not to try to conquer everything in a day— you'll only get overwhelmed and quit. Nor should you wait until the ideal time presents itself—it'll never hap-

> I'm not in competition with anybody but myself. My goal is to beat my last performance.
> *Celine Dion*

pen. The only way to reach your ultimate goal is to take baby steps every day. Some days the effort may be nothing more than squeezing in twenty minutes of practice, or making a phone call to follow up on a lead, but in time, these baby steps will add up to a huge leap. Understand that growth and progress don't always happen on a steady vertical incline. Sometimes it takes awhile to see results, but mark my words, you will.

One way to remind yourself to take a baby step every day is to write out your ultimate goal on a sheet of paper. Put it where you'll be sure to see it every day—like on the bathroom mirror or the dashboard of your car. It will help to keep you focused when life seems to get in the way. As long as you can take stock at the end of every day and see that in some small way you've done something to bring you closer to your goal, then you can pat yourself on the back and congratulate the diva within.

Diva Diary

It's amazing how powerful putting pen to paper can be for the purpose of reaching your goal, and that's why it is essential that you start a diva diary. Capturing your uncensored, spontaneous, or random thoughts, especially first thing in the morning, is often the key to finding the emotional and spiritual focus that may be missing. It doesn't have to be all positive either; writing down your misgivings and gripes is wonderfully cathartic and makes it easier to think positively throughout the rest of the day. Anything and everything that's on your mind—your dreams from the night before, a nagging thought that won't go away, or just stream-of-consciousness ramblings—is fit to print. Spending some private time once a day with your diva diary will help accelerate your momentum and crystalize your dream.

Diversity Is Key

As you set out to define your goal, you need to keep something in mind.

PRACTICAL GEM
Diversity is key to making a living as a full-time singer.

This may seem obvious, but I can't tell you how many vocalists I've met who will sing only one style of music or in one kind of venue, and then complain because they aren't working enough. I don't know if it's because they're snobbish and think their chosen music style or venue is better than any other, or if it's because they have a fear of learning unfamiliar songs or working in unfamiliar environments. Maybe they just have their heart set on singing one particular style of music, which then dictates the places they can perform. But whatever the reason, they suffer not only financially but also in their personal and professional growth. If you are willing to stay open-minded and sing many different styles of popular music—from soul, to country, to jazz, to Broadway, and everything in between—you will be in great demand, not to mention a better, more well-rounded vocalist. There are so many different venues and occasions for a variety of live music, and to disregard even one is to put yourself at a disadvantage—it's like cutting off a source of immediate and long-term income, not to mention a possible once-in-a-lifetime chance.

Fear of the Unknown

I'm reminded of the time I begrudgingly took a gig at a bookstore cafe. I wasn't looking forward to performing in an environment where people traditionally tend to get annoyed when you whisper, much less sing. And it was pretty much as I had predicted. A few people seemed to appreciate the music, but most who stuck around found a seat as far away as possible so they could read. I was vowing to never play a bookstore cafe again when a man approached with his card. He was a surgeon at the local hospital, liked the music, and asked if our band could perform at a party he was having—on his yacht! If that weren't enough, our band has been hired to perform at several hospital functions since. Fear of the unknown almost got the better of me, but I said yes in spite of them, and the rewards just keep on coming.

Say "Yes"

Just about every kind of experience can be valuable. I've learned something and/ or made contacts by per-

> Never, never listen to anybody when they try to discourage you; because they do that, believe me.
>
> *Mariah Carey*

forming poolside singing island music, at a bar mitzvah singing "Havah Nagilah," at a department store singing Christmas carols, and at a St. Patrick's Day celebration singing dozens of Irish ditties. In the studio, I've sung in the voice of a hillbilly fish (one of my better impersonations), a valley-girl cheerleader, and an Italian opera singer, just to name a few. I've donned costumes for theme parties and performed dressed as one of the Supremes, an Andrews Sister, and a poodle-skirted sock hopper. Are you starting to get the picture? I had little or no prior experience in any of these genres or situations, but I said yes anyway. More often than not, saying yes to the unfamiliar and staying open to what new experiences have to offer will increase not only your earning power but your diva power as well. You'll get another feather in your boa every time you dare!

Venues and Occasions for Live Music

- ❋ Bar, lounge, or nightclub
- ❋ Restaurant or cafe
- ❋ Fair, festival, or carnival
- ❋ Corporate event
- ❋ Store, plaza, or shopping mall promotion or grand opening
- ❋ Hotel
- ❋ Casino
- ❋ Theme/amusement park
- ❋ Charity event

✶ Cabaret
✶ Company party
✶ Cruise ship
✶ Dinner cruise
✶ Lodge or club
✶ Wedding
✶ Class reunion
✶ Bar or bat mitzvah
✶ Birthday, anniversary, or holiday celebration
✶ Recording studio

Beware of Naysayers

I'll warn you now that there will be plenty of naysayers to discourage you at every turn. Their reasons may be altruistic, or they may be selfish: They may fear that you'll fail miserably or simply be jealous of your chance at success. My mother is now one of my biggest cheerleaders. But there was a time when even she was so afraid I'd end up homeless by leaving my day job to sing full time that she was doubtful of my pursuit. And then there are those who seem to actually enjoy stomping on your dreams. Just think about it. If a certain kind of person sees you going after a dream, and he himself is stagnant and for whatever reason denying himself his own passion, that person is going to feel envious of your moxie. And rather than face his own personal void and then do the work required to fill it, it's going to be much easier for him to try and squash your enthusiasm by belittling your efforts. That way, he won't have to face his own failure in the mirror of your success.

The Bold and the Bitter

I stayed with my first band for four years, and although I benefited greatly from the experience, I had to contend with a major naysayer: the bandleader. He was an older man who constantly expressed blame and bitterness about not being farther along in his career.

Whenever I made the mistake of communicating any enthusiasm or hope for my own future singing career, he was quick to brush it aside as naiveté or just plain ignorance.

The Last Straw

I remember one particularly offensive incident because it was when I made up my mind to move on. An entertainment lawyer from New York approached me at the end of a gig with his business card and a lovely compliment on my voice. After we chatted a while, he asked if I would send him a demo to shop around, and this bandleader, who had nosily hung around within earshot, actually laughed out loud. The bandleader later told me that there was no way this lawyer was on the up and up, and that even if he were legitimate, I wasn't nearly ready for anything like what he was offering. I have to say that even with a strong support system of friends and family, I experienced a flood of self-doubt and considered not following through. (Naysayers always have the most damaging words in their arsenal to attack your self-esteem because a similar litany plays in their own heads constantly.) But anger at this bandleader for being so cruel was the overwhelming feeling I experienced, and I finally came to the conclusion that making a demo and mailing it off couldn't hurt anyone.

> "Don't ever mistrust those voices in your head.
> *Alanis Morissette*

Although nothing ever came of this deal, it did provide a much-needed ego boost after being with said bandleader for four years. It also gave me the push I needed to go into a professional recording studio for the first time to make a quality demo. Ultimately, that demo served to open many other doors to more lucrative and fulfilling jobs.

Significant Others

It is also quite common for an emerging diva's significant other to be especially threatened by her new direction and to don the naysayer's hat. Here you are, taking time away for practice and study that may eventually lead you to taking more time away to perform. Add that to the fact that when you do start performing, you'll be getting dressed to the nines and looking better than ever when you walk out the door for work, where you'll probably have a fair share of admirers. I've seen more than one relationship get rocky when a vocalist's career starts to take off.

To help smooth the transition, try to keep your partner involved in the process so he can witness how happy you are when you sing. Ask your sweetie pie to help you set up a practice space (described in chapter 2), or invite him to join you on your ongoing field trips (listed in chapter 3). When you begin singing in public, ask your little cupcake for valuable support by accompanying you to and cheering you on at karaoke night or an open mic night. And finally, try to convince your snookums that he is indispensable as a source for constructive criticism and a sounding board for making decisions every step of the way to divahood. Oh, yeah, and promise that in exchange for his support, you'll even stop calling him annoyingly cutsey pet names.

You Know What's Best for You

GOLDEN RULE
Never doubt the fact that you, and you alone, know what is best for you.

If someone in your life is not supportive of you following your dream (or is even downright discouraging), then you need to question *their* motives, not yours. You are the one who knows what it is that makes you excited about getting up in the morning, what puts that extra spring in your step. And to help keep you highly motivated and immune to all of the negative stuff, I suggest you find your own inspiring personal anthem. Pick a song by a great diva that urges you to be strong and persevere, one that encourages you to be fearless in the pursuit of your dreams, or one that just plain fires you up. And whenever you are faced with adversity of any kind, listen to your anthem loud and often.

My Favorite Diva Anthems

- ❊ Fantasia Barrino, "I Believe"
- ❊ Irene Cara, "What a Feeling"
- ❊ Mariah Carey, "Make It Happen"
- ❊ Destiny's Child, "Survivor"
- ❊ Dixie Chicks, "Wide Open Spaces"
- ❊ Aretha Franklin, "Respect"
- ❊ Peggy Lee, "I'm a Woman"
- ❊ Martina McBride, "Happy Girl"

Just Rewards

Playing your diva anthem will be an important gift you give yourself in times of need—and in keeping with the effectiveness of positive reinforcement, I also want you to come up with a personal reward plan for when you've gotten over a hurdle or made significant progress. I've noticed that many of my voice students rarely look back to see how far they've come, but rather, they are always looking ahead at what more they need to do to reach their goals. This kind of thinking only breeds frustration and sometimes futility. To avoid burnout and to help keep that initial energizing enthusiasm, you need to congratulate yourself with a treat for every milestone. Your rewards may change over time from a manicure now to a quality vocal microphone down the road, but the important thing is for you to acknowledge a job well done. No one thrives when they feel unappreciated. The following exercise should help to get you started.

The Diva Readiness Exercise

In order to make a real life change, you need to get fully prepared with a well-thought-out plan of action. By filling in the blanks below with some concrete objectives, you will help to solidify your goal.

- I want to start making my dream a reality by ______________ ______________________________. *(Fill in a realistic short-term goal of breaking one counterproductive habit. For example: "removing the words 'I can't' from my vocabulary.")*
- In five years, I see myself ____________________________ ____. *(Insert your ultimate goal, and be as specific as you can.)*
- To prepare myself immediately, I need to ______________ ______________________, ________________________, and ______________________________________. *(List three things you can do right now. For example: "start a diva diary.")*
- It's very possible that ________________________________ ____, ____, and ____, but I'll be ready for them by__________________________________, _________________________, and ____________________ ____. *(Name three potential pitfalls and three strategies for avoiding them. For example: "So and so will try to dissuade me from following my dream"/"refraining from discussing my plans with that person.")*
- In order to make a huge leap of progress toward my goal, I need to take baby steps every day by _____________________ ____, ____________________________________, and _________ ____ ___________________________. *(Vocal practice has to be one, but think of two more.)*

✤ Whenever I reach a milestone, I plan to treat myself with
_____, _____, or
_____. (*List your top three indulgences.*
For example: "a massage.")

A Good Start

You have a lot of work in front of you, and in order to greet each day
with the energy and enthusiasm necessary for your diva training,
breakfast is imperative. Skip this meal, and I am convinced you will
set the tone for the whole day: "I don't care enough about myself to
provide nourishment to my body upon waking, to spend some quiet
time with my diva diary, to coordinate my day to include vocal practice, or to believe I am worth all the effort. . . ." Give yourself every
advantage to succeed by starting each day with a good breakfast.

Oatmeal has never been one of my favorite breakfast items, but
I decided to find a way to prepare this heart-healthy food so it would
taste less like the mush I remembered from childhood. The results of
my experimentation have far exceeded my expectations, and I think
you'll agree that this oatmeal ain't like your mama used to make.

TASTY TIDBIT: OVERTURE OATMEAL
- ✤ *1 cup vanilla soy milk*
- ✤ *½ cup old fashioned oatmeal*
- ✤ *¼ cup walnuts, chopped*
- ✤ *½ cup apples, peeled and chopped*
- ✤ *1 teaspoon cinnamon*

*Cook oatmeal according to package directions, adding walnuts
and apples when you add oatmeal to boiling milk. Stir in cinnamon right before serving. (For a yummy variation, prepare the oatmeal with only the vanilla soy milk according to package
directions, transfer to a serving bowl, and stir in two tablespoons of
peanut butter.)*

To Sum It Up

diva (*n*): a woman who is, above all else, passionate. She finds what she truly desires in life and patiently, persistently goes after it. She is willing to take risks, to put herself out front in the spotlight; sometimes she will shine, and sometimes the bright lights will serve only to illuminate her mistakes. But she understands that she'll never flourish while hiding in the dark.

Above is my definition of a diva and my creed through the years when I've doubted myself, felt overwhelmed with the work ahead of me, or been overcome with negativity from others. In this chapter, my goal has been to help you become mentally focused and prepare you for the inevitable setbacks, obstacles, and detours, so that when, not if, they happen to you, you'll be prepared and able to persevere.

A DIVA NEXT DOOR SAYS . . .

I was married to a man for twenty years who repeatedly told me, "Don't think that you can get up in front of an audience and sing. You're not nearly as good as you think you are." When he left the scene, a difficult year followed, but I kept these words in mind: "When God closes a door, he opens a window." They helped tremendously as I struggled to regain my independence and self-esteem and pursue my lifelong dream to sing. So many times it seemed that I'd come to the end of my possibilities when agents didn't return phone calls or a promising gig fell through. And then, out of the blue, a contact called back, and I was performing within a year of my divorce. — Nanci

CHAPTER 2

Sing, Sing a Song

GETTING (AND KEEPING) YOUR VOICE

IN SHAPE FOR THE STAGE

S inging is easy. Just picture a kindergarten class belting out "Itsy Bitsy Spider," and you'll understand what I mean. Children don't think about how they're singing; they just do it because it's fun, and the results are strong, self-assured voices, filled with the sheer joy of the process. Unfortunately, this skill, which comes so naturally to us as kids, can get lost as we grow up.

Vocal Hitches

Some of us lose our skill to sing when fear—a singer's worst enemy— sets in. Fear of looking silly, fear of making a mistake, fear of not setting the world on fire with the first note, fear of failing miserably —these thoughts handicap a singer the moment they enter her mind. Between the shortness of breath, tightening of the throat, and tense

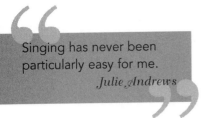

Singing has never been
particularly easy for me.
Julie Andrews

body muscles caused by fear, the singing voice doesn't stand a chance. Believe it or not, singing is a largely mental endeavor, and even if you are the most technically gifted singer on the planet, you can be crippled by fear.

Cheap Imitation

Fear isn't the only obstacle you will have to face on your road from point A to point Diva. Many times a singer will force notes, trying to manipulate her voice in an attempt to sound like her favorite singer on the radio or in her CD collection. I confess that for awhile, I made this mistake by trying to imitate one of my idols, Celine Dion. What was I thinking? The woman sings like an angel—she is a vocal freak of nature. Yet here I was, an alto (and a mere mortal no less), straining to do vocal gymnastics and reach notes in the stratosphere. Not only was this bad for my morale (I sounded like I was in labor), but it was also bad for the health of my voice and counterproductive to finding and appreciating my own unique qualities as a singer.

Cherish forever what makes you unique, because you're really a yawn if it goes.
Bette Midler

Always in the Chorus, Never a Soloist

A singer can also fall into what I call the "always in the chorus, never a soloist" syndrome. Don't get me wrong—being in a chorus is a wonderful opportunity to learn theory and harmony, sight reading, and performance skills. But because of a choral group's very nature, the singer is encouraged to use her head voice to blend in and sound as one with the others in her section. When the singer then sings solo, her voice can sound airy and shallow, with no presence or individuality.

Lockjawed and Tongue-Tied

Sometimes the only real hindrance for a singer is that she doesn't understand that talking and singing are two different activities. The singer mistakenly uses the same effort and enunciation she uses to talk when she sings, and so she doesn't open up her mouth wide enough and lazily rolls out words. This doesn't allow for a clear, full sound, and can even contribute to pitch problems.

Out of Style

And finally, even a great voice can sound downright silly if the vocal styling doesn't match the musical genre. I was once made painfully aware of this mistake when I saw a singer jazz-scatting through a country-and-western song. I don't know if she was purposely trying to experiment, in which case her performance might have been more appropriate in a coffee house rather than a hotel lounge. Maybe she was trying to show off her scatting ability in what would otherwise have been a simple song to sing. But the effect of her performance on the audience was one of puzzlement and mild amusement.

For an even more extreme example, think how ridiculous a classical soprano voice like that of Julie Andrews would sound singing a funky R&B song like Destiny's Child's "Bootylicious." Sounds like a *Saturday Night Live* skit, right? Pop music has plenty of room for individuality. But there are a few rules for singing pop music that when broken, can have you unwittingly turning your performance into a musical comedy.

Help Is on the Way

First, fear not. It's much easier said than done, I know. Fear was one of the greatest obstacles I had to overcome when I began singing. There came a time after the ignorant bliss of young childhood when I didn't even want to practice singing at home if anyone was in the house. Every solo I ever tried out for in the school chorus was a total disaster, due to my fear. But it eventually became apparent that my behavior wasn't consistent with what I was working toward: to sing beautifully in front of people. So I made a very conscious decision that I was not going to let fear get the best of me.

Face Your Fear

The fact is, the only way to conquer your fear is to face it a little bit at a time. Try to determine when in your life the fear kicked in and why. At some point, did somebody make an insensitive or negative comment about your voice? Were you always labeled by everyone as the "shy one"? Does the idea prevail in your family that musical pursuits should strictly be a hobby? It's amazing how events and attitudes that seem so small in childhood can set us up for a lifetime of dissatisfaction and unfulfilled dreams.

Work through It

I started working through my fear by singing in front of my family. This prepared me for the next step, which was sitting in at "open mic" nights and eventually going for an audition. The weekly practices with a band prepared me for the next step, which was performing in public. And each performance since has taught me how to better control my fear and even use it as a motivator. I get angry at my fear when it rears its ugly head, and I vow to show it who's boss by challenging myself. You might try role-playing. To help you work through your jitters, pretend you're a singer whom you admire, and remember that even the biggest singing stars in the world deal with fear.

Breathe

Diaphragmatic breathing is the energy source from which every beautiful note is sung. Everyone knows how to breathe, but most people's everyday breathing is the shallow version of the real thing. While it's adequate for talking, it won't sustain a vocalist for very long.

Go ahead, take a deep breath now. If you're raising your shoulders and puffing out your chest, then you aren't filling even a smidgen of your lungs' capacity, and you aren't breathing from your diaphragm.

> If I hold back, I'm no good now, and I'd rather be good sometimes than holding back all the time.
> *Janis Joplin*

BREATHING EXERCISES

When you breathe correctly for singing, the respiratory effort is done by the abdominal muscles, which causes your stomach to swell as you inhale and to shrink as you sing. For many, this feels awkward or even backwards at first, so here's a great exercise that will reinforce proper breathing habits. Turn sideways while looking in a full-length mirror. On a count of ten, inhale through your nose with first the stomach and then the chest filling to maximum capacity. Then steadily release the air, singing "hee" on any comfortable note. Be sure to use your stomach muscles to push out every last bit of air. It helps to put your hand on your belly to make sure it is moving out when you inhale and in when you sing "hee." After repeating this exercise several times, your abdominal muscles should feel slightly fatigued, as if you've done some sit-ups.

This second breathing exercise is a variation of the same technique, and it may drive home the concept of using the abdominal muscles to breathe even more strongly. It requires that you lie on your back on the floor with your knees bent and your arms by your sides. Balance a small, light object on your stomach (this book would work perfectly). Now breathe deeply through your nose, filling up your lungs for as long as possible: as you do so, the book should rise toward the ceiling. Now as you exhale, singing "hee," the book should sink down on your stomach toward the floor. As you breathe in and out, visualize an inner tube around your stomach inflating and deflating.

TRICK OF THE TRADE
Toned abs are the bonus payoff for these breathing exercises.

ANYWHERE, ANYTIME

You can even practice diaphragmatic breathing while driving in your car, watching TV, or doing housework. You want this way of breathing to become second nature so that eventually you don't have to focus on the process while you're singing. Your body will love all the extra oxygen you're providing, and your mind will feel the stress-relieving effects.

Placement

The proper placement for singing pop music is primarily the chest voice. Placement refers to the area where the air is resonating and the tone that results. Rather than my showing you a complicated diagram illustrating airflow from the vocal cords through the nasal cavity and mouth—since I myself could never quite decipher that diagram—I'll ask you to sing "Happy Birthday." Sing it like you did when you were six years old at your best friend's party and happy as hell that cake and ice cream were on the way. Or sing "We Will Rock You" as if you were in a crowded stadium, caught up in the spirit of cheering on your favorite team. Pretend that you want to get someone's attention across a crowded and noisy room, and then sing "Hey!" in the bold and confident manner that you would use in that situation. Singing with childlike abandon and a sense of play are sure ways to find your chest voice in order to produce controlled yelling, which is all singing really is.

> " I'm lucky enough to have a chest voice for pop as well as a head [voice] for opera.
> *Sarah Brightman* "

Styling

Now that you've found the proper placement, you have to make sure you are using the appropriate styling for pop music. This can be a difficult concept to grasp and even more difficult to conquer, especially for those whose background is predominately choral, those with a heavy vibrato, or those who were brought up listening to only one or two kinds of music. The best way for me to describe pop styling is that it's somewhere between the twang of a down-home country singer and the formal affectation of a classical vocalist.

Here's a quick exercise that should clarify. Look in the mirror and sing the word "love." Notice that if you keep your mouth nearly closed when you sing, it comes out sounding like "luv," which is too country. If you open your mouth very wide when you sing, it comes out sounding like "lahv," which is too classical. Now drop your jaw so that your mouth is open but not to the point of being uncomfortable. When you sing "love," it should sound the way most people in our country say it. In other words, pop songs should be sung in the pop(ular) vernacular.

Vibrato

Controlling your vibrato is also imperative so that you don't sound like the character on that *Saturday Night Live* skit I described earlier. Turn on the radio and start going through the stations from adult contemporary to contemporary country to jazz to Top Forty. Notice how the artists generally sing straight notes, only allowing their vibrato to come through at the end of a word or a phrase. If you start to pay attention to the phrasing and the diction, you'll see that there are variations between different styles of pop music and different singers, but overall there is a norm in the amount of vibrato used.

Your Mouth

In order to sing, your mouth needs to be open and your tongue out of the way so that the sound you're creating has an unobstructed path and therefore can be clearly heard. Look in the mirror and yawn. See how your tongue is flat against the bottom of your mouth and behind your bottom teeth. Also notice how the back of your throat is in the shape of an *o* and you can see that little punching bag, or the uvula, hanging there. This is the way your mouth should be when you sing.

Now you may still be wondering how it is possible to keep this good form when you are actually singing. It isn't as hard as it may seem. While looking in the mirror, drop your jaw and place your index finger on your chin not allowing it to move. Now repeatedly sing "lah-gah" on any comfortable note. Your jaw shouldn't be moving, only your tongue. Now try "pah-mah." This time your jaw has to move slightly so that you can form the consonants *p* and *m*, but the goal is to just touch on the consonants and then quickly open your mouth again. This exercise can be done with any combination of a consonant and vowel, like "toe-roe" or "noo-foo," etc. The purpose, of course, is to reinforce the good singing habit of quickly touching on consonants so that the mouth remains open as much as possible, thereby making it possible to produce clear, unmuffled sound.

If you ever have the chance, rent the 1990 movie *Dick Tracy* costarring Madonna. At the very beginning of the film, there is a close-up of her mouth as she sings the song "Sooner or Later," and her technique is flawless.

Staying in Tune

It used to be widely believed that tone deafness was hereditary, and therefore a person was either born with a "good ear" or not. Some studies now indicate that healthy babies are born with perfect pitch, and keeping perfect pitch may be more a matter of using it or losing it. I tend to believe this view because through consistent practice, I've heard vast improvement in myself and others.

LONG TONES

A simple yet effective exercise that maintains and eventually improves your ability to sing a note in tune is called long tones. This involves playing a single note (middle C is a good place to start) on a keyboard or piano, and then singing that note as "ah." Try to concentrate and really zero in on the note mentally before you vocalize. Use your ears to find the center of pitch. I've noticed when giving voice lessons that if I tell a student who is having trouble to stop and take time to purposefully listen before vocalizing, she is better able to sing in tune.

As you sing "ah," make it as smooth and steady as possible, allowing no vibrato or wavering on and off pitch, until you run out of air. Once you've continued up the scale for at least one octave, push yourself a little, and sing the next few notes that are beyond your top and bottom range. These notes in your upper and lower registers may feel weak, uncomfortable, or even strained today, but with practice, they can eventually become a part of your range.

Practice

As with anything, practice makes perfect. I am still amazed at how even a small amount of practice can positively affect my performances. (And boy, do I know when I slip!) You, too, will quickly begin to see the benefits of committing to a consistent practice schedule. Remember your ultimate goal, and know that even if you can only fit a short practice into your day, you're still moving in the right direction.

Practice Journal

Keeping a journal is a great way to increase productivity. While your diva diary is for your mental, emotional, and spiritual growth and well-being, the practice journal is for—you guessed it—the practical aspects of singing.

Begin by writing down some reasonable goals at the beginning of each week, and then check them off as you complete them. Everyone has different times of the day when her energy levels peak. By recording the time of day you practice and jotting down some thoughts on your physical and mental state, over time, you'll get to know what time of day works best for you and how environmental factors play a role.

By doing this in my own practice schedules, I've gathered some helpful information. For instance, I have noticed that if I practice immediately following some aerobic exercise in the morning, I have more energy and power. I've also discovered that drinking a fruit smoothie before my practice will make it feel like the notes are stuck in my throat and that eating a handful of almonds causes me to cough when I try to sing. Note to self: Don't eat nuts or drink a smoothie before practice. These journal notes will be equally helpful in making the most of your practice time.

Practice Space

You'll be much more likely to stick to a daily practice schedule if you've created a space for that sole purpose. Furthermore, taking the time and energy to carve out an area, even if it's a corner of the room, and designating it as your practice space, is a concrete way to show yourself and perhaps others that you are serious about pursuing your passion to sing. You will need a keyboard or a piano, a full-length mirror, a sound system with recording capacity, and a small table for items such as your journal, water bottle, etc.

The Warm-Up

To keep your practice times simple and efficient, I recommend combining the aforementioned breathing, placement, and long tone exercises into a twenty-minute warm-up before you begin singing.

✳ Stand in front of the mirror with your arms by your side, knees slightly bent, and your shoulders and neck muscles relaxed.
✳ Roll your head from side to side to release any tension.
✳ Place one hand on your stomach to make sure you're breathing properly throughout the exercise—stomach goes out when you inhale and goes in when you sing.
✳ Play middle C on the piano, close your eyes, and put your full attention on hearing the note.
✳ Take a deep breath, and sing "ah" in your strong chest voice, allowing no vibrato.

- Hold the note for as long as you can sustain it, making sure your jaw is dropped.
- Continue up the scale at least one octave.

Vocalizing

> What's important is to stand out there with your legs planted apart and sing, dammit.
>
> *Liza Minelli*

Spend the next twenty minutes working on a song for your repertoire. Choose a song and then listen to a recording by a great singer over and over again, becoming familiar enough with the melody so that you can sing it without the recording. Write or type out the lyrics, and judging by the length of the phrases, natural pauses, and your personal lung capacity, mark a small *x* as a reminder for where you need to take breaths throughout the song.

EXAMPLE WITH *HAPPY BIRTHDAY* . . .
(x) *Happy birthday to you,* (x) *happy birthday to you,* (x) *happy birthday, happy birthday,* (x) *happy birthday to you* (x).

Now slowly sing the song a capella, line by line, listening carefully for any problem areas. Don't continue with the song until you have dissected the problem area and figured out the hitch (e.g., improper placement, insufficient air, too much vibrato, etc.). In other words, don't keep singing the song from start to finish and think that you're achieving a quality vocal practice. It's quite possible that in your first session, you may only get as far as the first line of the song. Try not to get frustrated if it takes some time, and remember that each song has several potential lessons. If you take the time to master a line before moving on, you aren't likely to make that particular mistake again—there or in any song you sing thereafter.

Home Recording

And finally, record your practice once a week. This serves two purposes. You'll be better able to measure your technical progress from week to week—that is, your breath control, tone recognition, etc. Also, you'll begin the vital process of falling in love with the sound of your own unique voice. At first, the recordings may trouble you because they don't sound the way your favorite singer sounds or the way you think a beautiful female voice should sound. But I'm hoping that over time you'll embrace that which distinguishes your voice from every other singer out there. Only then can you sing from a place of confidence and joy, thereby achieving true artistry. Just think of the loss to society if Ricki Lee Jones, Stevie Nicks, Billie Holiday, or Macy Gray had tried to change her voice to fit some ideal or had felt discouraged and quit altogether. It would have been a sad day, indeed!

> "Some of the most wonderful people are the ones who don't fit into boxes.
> *Tori Amos*"

Study

Practice doesn't always have to involve actual singing. In fact, too much singing can lead to any number of voice problems, as I'll explain later in this chapter. You can still be improving on your skills when you're not singing, however, by listening to great singers, memorizing the lyrics of the song on which you are working, or listening to your recorded practice and making notes. Quiet study is one more way to improve upon your craft.

Further Instruction

You may feel the need for further guidance in your vocal training to learn additional vocal exercises, reinforce proper technique, or gain some basic music-theory knowledge. There are several helpful books and videos available, which I list at the end of this book. Or you may want to find a voice coach. Keep in mind that you don't need a classical voice coach if you are studying pop music, so interview a few teachers before you commit to anyone. Make sure the teacher you choose has experience teaching rock, country, R&B, and jazz music, and tell her your particular goals. If you don't do this, your lessons may end up being useless or even counterproductive.

PRACTICAL GEM
Once you've found the right teacher, ask permission to record your lessons. You'll cut down on the number of lessons needed and have a permanent reference if you ever need a refresher course.

I, myself, have always believed that the best teachers in the world are as close as your personal music collection. Growing up, I didn't have access to a voice teacher or instructional videos, but I did have Ella, and Patsy, and Aretha, and Liza, and Barbra, and many more greats to listen to and absorb. These divas were infinitely patient in their tutelage, allowing me to listen to them for hours and sing along to my heart's content.

A Healthy Voice

Learning to sing properly will not only make you sound better, but it will also insure your career's longevity by keeping your voice strong and healthy. Take the time now to learn how to warm up and to sing from your diaphragm so that you won't be faced with throat problems down the road. These problems can range from laryngitis to the much more serious consequences of developing vocal nodes or polyps. These are caused by vocal misuse and abuse and may require surgery, which could then result in a permanent loss of range and tonal quality—not something any singer wants to deal with.

Lifestyle

Even when you aren't singing, take good care of your voice by avoiding yelling or screaming, excessive whispering and throat clearing, coughing, and smoking. Look at your lifestyle carefully to see if there are areas in which you could save your voice. If, for instance, you've always enjoyed talking to your friends on the phone for hours, then you might want to start curtailing that a bit. If you're in the admittedly enjoyable habit of singing at the top of your lungs as you zoom down the highway, listen to an audio book instead. Or perhaps you regularly engage in probably the most damaging of all pastimes for a singer: simultaneously smoking, drinking alcohol, and talking in a noisy establishment. Such an environment literally tortures your vocal cords, as you first dehydrate them with smoke and alcohol and then strain them by trying to talk over the boisterous crowd.

Moderation

Now I know that it's starting to sound like you have to live like a nun in order to maintain a healthy voice. But it's really about becoming more aware of your everyday activities and how they'll affect your instrument, and then doing these things in moderation. You're now using your voice more for singing practice, so make concessions in other areas so you don't tax those treasured vocal cords.

Water

TASTY TIDBIT
Sipping room-temperature water throughout your practice is the best way to keep your voice hydrated and sounding strong.

Tepid water may sound awfully bland, but other than herbal tea with honey, there are really no other options. When you're singing for any length of time, it is absolutely necessary to keep your throat moist for optimum results. The caffeine in coffee or black tea will dehydrate you, causing your throat to get dry, and most sodas also contain caffeine plus carbonation, which causes you to burp. Milk is no good either, because it tends to cause a mucus buildup in the throat. So the easiest and best habit is to keep a water bottle handy whenever you sing and then take sips regularly.

Fending Off Colds

For most people, a cold is nothing more than a minor inconvenience that requires some over-the-counter medicine in order to get on with the day. Any member of a band, from the drummer to the bass player, could show up to a gig and perform just fine with a cold. For a vocalist, however, a cold targets her voice, which means that at best she can't practice and her performance is severely hindered, and at worst, she is looking at a couple of days of an unpaid leave of absence. Suffice it to say, it is worth using every precaution to avoid getting one of these nasty buggers.

Obviously I'm not a doctor, but I am a walking science experiment when it comes to cold prevention. Over the years, I've consulted nutritionists, books, the Internet, my physician, and the staff of my local health-food store, and I've tried just about everything to avoid the dreaded tickle at the back of my throat that signals a cold. Of course, the best defense is a healthy immune system, so I always try to get plenty of sleep, take my multivitamin capsule, drink lots of water, and eat and drink several of the foods known to contain antioxidants.

TASTY TIDBIT: WELLNESS FARE

❊ *Green tea*
❊ *Brightly colored fresh fruits and vegetables*
❊ *A variety of nuts, beans, legumes, and seeds*
❊ *Fish and shellfish*
❊ *Red wine (one glass a day)*
❊ *Dark chocolate that contains 85 percent cocoa*

At the First Sign of a Cold

Sometimes if I'm overworked and stressed out, however, my body can't fight off the germs on its own. The remedies I've tried have included everything from an old Mexican recipe for tea infused with so much fresh garlic that it made me cry (and stink to high heaven), to the more conventional prescription of massive doses of vitamin C. Listed below are what I've found to be the most effective remedies to use at the first sign of a cold. As with all supplements and medications, read the labels carefully before taking.

Nip-It-in-the-Bud Cold Remedies

❊ Immediately start using Zicam Cold Remedy, a homeopathic, over-the-counter nasal spray, which lessens the severity and duration of a cold.
❊ Take a combination echinacea-and-goldenseal supplement to support the body's natural defenses.
❊ Use a humidifier in your home.
❊ Drink plenty of water with lemon.
❊ Sip green tea infused with fresh ginger, lemon, and honey.

And if you're really desperate, drink a cup of tomato juice mixed with a large clove of fresh minced garlic and the juice from one fresh lemon.

Singing with a Cold

If it happens that you do have to sing with a cold and/or cough, here are my recommendations to get you through the gig in as functional a manner as possible. Of course, resting the voice for the duration of the cold would be ideal, but such is the life of a professional vocalist.

Get-through-the-Gig Aids

❊ Saline nasal spray
❊ Contac Cold decongestant caplets (non-drowsy formula)

✣ Robitussin expectorant cough syrup (single ingredient Guaifenesin—green label)
✣ Slippery-elm throat lozenge
✣ Fenugreek tea with honey

A Word from Mark Widick, M.D.

I asked my friend, Dr. Mark Widick—an ear, nose, and throat specialist who studied at the world-renowned Vanderbilt University Voice Center—what he would prescribe for an ailing vocalist who wanted to perform and when he would recommend that a vocalist absolutely not sing. Here is what he had to say:

> There is always some risk when a vocalist sings with a sore throat or hoarse voice that it will exacerbate the problem. With that said, I know that professional vocalists sometimes need to perform even when sick. Upon examination of the throat, if I find that it is a case of laryngitis, I may administer a cortisone shot to reduce inflammation, but recommend that the patient rest the voice as soon as possible after the performance. If I find the beginnings of nodules or polyps, or evidence of bleeding in the throat, then I would highly recommend that the patient cancel the performance, rest the voice completely, and do some further testing. Only after evaluation for gastric reflux disease in which the stomach acid rises into the throat and burns the vocal cords, and exhausting noninvasive treatments like voice coaching and speech therapy would surgery be recommended.

To Sum It Up

In order to build a strong and healthy singing voice, you have to go back to the basics. In this chapter, I have provided descriptions of the most common problems a singer will encounter, along with simple exercises, activities, and an efficient practice regimen to help overcome them. It is important to be brutally honest with yourself and willing to face head-on any problems you may have with both the physical and mental aspects of singing. Once you've identified your weaknesses, only time and consistent practice will enable you to break old habits, learn new skills, and make the lifestyle changes necessary to get your voice in diva shape, thereby making singing the joyful process it was meant to be.

A DIVA NEXT DOOR SAYS
Confidence is very important when singing. If you are unsure of yourself and think you can't do it, chances are you won't be able to. I had a real hard time with this recently. I had decided it was time to move in a different direction from the band that I was in. I gave the bandleader ample notice to find a replacement, but he was angry about my decision nonetheless. From then on, he told me I was singing flat all the time, and even though I knew where his motivation to cut me down was coming from, it totally undermined my confidence. I was so stressed in his presence that I actually began to sing flat, and the vicious cycle continued until I finally left. Now I'm in a band with great musicians who are also friends, and my confidence and career are better than ever. —Fonda

CHAPTER 3

I'm Coming Out

VENTURING INTO YOUR
LOCAL MUSIC SCENE

I n addition to practicing every day, you need to start venturing out into your local music scene, and that means taking some ongoing field trips. There's no time like the present, even if you feel like you're still a beginner and that any public display of interest is premature. These field trips are necessary for your well-rounded diva education, as you are going to establish contacts and build relationships with people in the business, learn more about the inner workings

> The sad truth is that opportunity doesn't knock twice. You can put things off until tomorrow, but tomorrow may never come.
>
> *Gloria Estefan*

of a band, and discover new sources of inspiration to keep you motivated and moving forward toward your goal.

Live Music Venues

The first of these field trips is to go and see live music in your area. Make it a point to go as often as possible and to as many different venues as you can find. There are innumerable lessons to be learned by observing a band, but there are some main areas you should pay particular attention to.

Main Areas to Observe in Live Performance

✳ Stage presence
✳ Use of performance space
✳ Repertoire
✳ Patter (talk between songs)
✳ Wardrobe
✳ Audience response
✳ Lighting

Be sure to take notes in a small notebook of what dazzled you; these notes will come in handy later when you're putting together your own song list, developing your personal style, and "packaging" your act—and yourself—for the public.

If only I had done this before my first gig. I was told that it was a formal affair and to dress appropriately. Now, I think deep down I knew what that really meant for a performer, but another part of me thought that I couldn't possibly be so bold as to walk into this Small-town, U.S.A., shindig dressed as a singing star. Since it was only my first real gig, I thought it would somehow be presumptuous. So I played it safe and settled on wearing my best navy blue dress and pearls. After the gig, the bandleader suggested we go see another band that was performing down the road. The moment we walked in the club I spotted the lead singer. She was resplendent in her silver-sequined mini, and I knew I should have been so bold.

Watch for What Doesn't Work

Not only can you see what does work by watching others entertain, you can see what doesn't. I'll give you an example. I remember going to see a highly regarded husband-and-wife duo perform at a fancy hotel. Although they were both seasoned professionals and very talented, they were obviously in the midst of a fight. They wouldn't even look at each other during their performance, and the negative energy made me so uncomfortable that I couldn't enjoy their music. I had no idea until then how unprofessional and counterproductive bad vibes onstage could be for a band. I learned a valuable lesson that night.

GOLDEN RULE
Keep your problems, bad moods, issues with other band members, and anything else negative off the stage.

SLOPPY BUT SINCERE

This point was driven even further home to me when I went to see a folksinger in an oyster bar. She was accompanying herself on guitar, and although the quality of her singing and playing was pretty sloppy, her delivery was heartfelt and sincere. The joy and enthusiasm she obviously felt in making music was contagious, and it turned out to be a thoroughly enjoyable and entertaining evening. That being said, not only can a negative vibe diminish a highly talented performer, but I'd go so far as to say that a positive attitude and genuine approach can make a technically challenged performer sparkle. This discovery came as a real comfort to me when I first started performing in public, because I knew that if I allowed the joy I felt to shine through, it would compensate for any less-than-perfect skills.

Networking

Going to see live music serves another purpose. The working musicians and singers in any given area are likely to either know each other or have some working history together. They may have met at the music store, they might have been hired to perform together on a club date (a gig where musicians show up unrehearsed and either read music charts provided by the bandleader or just wing it), or they might have done studio work together. By supporting bands at various places around town and becoming familiar with names and personalities, you can start placing yourself in a positive light among the players. Before you know it, you'll have a network of supportive contacts even before you're ready to debut. Take notes in your notebook of the people you meet, or take a business card if it's available, so you'll be able to remember names—key for building business relationships.

Inspiration

Perhaps most importantly, going to see live music is inspiring! There's no question that at this point, it's going to be hard to stay motivated because you probably have yet to form a band, and there's no definite gig that you're working toward. But you'll be reminded quickly why you're putting in all those hours of practice and preparation if you see before you a person doing exactly what you would love to be doing. And I'm willing to bet that after seeing some live entertainment, you'll approach your practice with renewed enthusiasm.

Air Quality

One last note regarding the live music scene and air quality—unless it is a smoke-free environment, limit your time there. The threat of cigarette and cigar smoke to your vocal cords and your overall health cannot be overstated. I've never been a smoker, but because of the years I've spent singing and breathing secondhand smoke in live music venues, I have suffered ailments more common in a smoker, and my doctor still isn't convinced that I never light up. Thank goodness many states, including mine, are passing laws that require businesses to put the smoking area outside. But unless this is the case in your state, protect your voice and your health by sitting in the nonsmoking section and limiting your time in smoky environments.

The Video/DVD Store

Now get down to your local video/DVD store and pick up a live performance video by one of your favorite divas. You can view to your heart's content the elements of a great performance. And again, take notes. Every diva will have things she does in concert that you'll want to take away and somehow incorporate into your act. For instance, as a grand entrance, you may not be able to float in from the back of the stadium perched on a suspended stage. But you can begin a song from the back of the room using a wireless microphone, and slowly make your way through the audience to join the band onstage for a similarly dramatic effect.

Don't be tempted to forgo this field trip by turning on your favorite music television channel. For one thing, every video won't be of a live concert situation, which is where you'll be able to pick up performance tips, and for another, frankly there is just too much junk amongst the jewels. You can be much more discriminating and make better use of your time by renting one carefully selected video.

Must-See Diva-in-Concert Videos

* ❋ Barbra Streisand—*Timeless*
* ❋ Beyonce—*Live at Wembley*
* ❋ Cher—*Live in Concert*
* ❋ Faith Hill—*When the Lights Go Down*
* ❋ Janet Jackson—*The Velvet Rope Tour*
* ❋ Madonna—*The Girlie Show*
* ❋ Mariah Carey—*MTV Unplugged*
* ❋ VH1 *Divas Live* (any year)

Snack Time

If you're anything like me, TV time often means snack time. But before you go and get all cozy with that bag of chips or cookies, opt for a healthier choice like a fruit smoothie. You are beginning a new chapter in your life, and in order to stay firmly committed to your goal and make real changes, a holistic approach that includes your mental, emotional, spiritual, and physical attention is required. I'll talk more about the physical aspect and the importance of exercise and a healthy diet to your singing career in chapter 4, but for now, skip the junk food and enjoy your diva video with one of these Superstar Smoothies.

TASTY TIDBIT: SUPERSTAR SMOOTHIE

❉ *1 ripe banana, peeled, sliced, and frozen*
❉ *2 tablespoons natural peanut butter*
❉ *1 (6 oz.) container low-fat vanilla yogurt*
❉ *½ teaspoon honey*
❉ *2 tablespoons skim milk*

Mix all ingredients in a blender until smooth.

The Musical Instrument and Equipment Store

The next field trip is to go where musicians meet—that's right, the musical instrument and equipment store (which I refer to as just the "music store" from here on in). Just by making a monthly stop and browsing around, you can further broaden your network of those in the biz. More times than not, the salespeople are musicians and privy to all sorts of helpful information, like where bands are performing and who might be looking for a singer. You're also sure to run into other working musicians in the store, browsing and buying gear. It never hurts to approach the person checking out a guitar or testing a keyboard and asking her if she plays in a band. I can assure you that most people will be more than happy to share their music story.

Ask Questions

Start to familiarize yourself with the tools of the trade by asking questions of the sales staff. Microphones and the components of a P.A. (public address) system like the mixing board and monitors are just a few of the gadgets you'll need to have at least some working knowledge of when you begin performing. Ask questions, try out a few microphones, price music and mic stands. And to make sure your salesperson is most helpful, let him know that you'll soon be in the market to buy some of these items.

Buy a Shaker

Before you leave, purchase a small, hand-held, shaker-type percussion instrument. The plastic variety is very inexpensive and comes in all kinds of silly shapes and bright colors—hey, as that wise nanny Mary Poppins knew, it always helps to add an element of fun. I'll explain in chapter 5 how the shaker will be instrumental (pun intended) in developing your rhythmic feel for various styles of music, and eventually a visual and musical plus for your performances.

Online Music Communities and Resources

Go on the Web in search of an online music community or resource. The better local sites often provide chat rooms for meeting area singers and musicians, forums for the discussion of relevant topics, classified sections for buying and selling musical equipment, as well as jam session and work opportunities. "Mommy bands" are forming in communities all over the United States. These bands are usually made up of stay-at-home moms who also want to use their musical talents and make their own money. If this fits your description, an online community may be just the place to find such a group. The best sites enable you to have a finger on the pulse of the music scene in your area without even leaving the house.

If you don't have any luck accessing a good local site, check out Gig Finder (*www.gigfinder.com*) and Broadjam (*www.broadjam .com*). Both are international musician's services where you can always find something of interest, and once you're ready, you might even find the perfect job. Two of the best resources on the Net specifically for vocalists are the Singing Spot (*www.thesingingspot.com*) and Vocalist (*www.vocalist.org.uk*). These Web sites have loads of helpful information, articles, message boards, and links. And while you're surfing the Web, stop by the Diva Next Door (*www.thedivanextdoor.net*). Yours truly has created an online pop vocalist sorority with a monthly column, even more inside scoop and helpful hints, as well as a forum to dish with sisters.

The Library or Bookstore

Go to the library or bookstore, and get your hands on an inspiring diva biography. Reading a great vocalist's life story is like discovering a recipe for success. You can learn what the many ingredients are and how the assembling of those ingredients affected this diva's career at different stages. When I read about the incredible obstacles that some of my idols have overcome, I am encouraged and reenergized. It's inevitable that we're all going to make our own mistakes, but if we can avoid just one pitfall by learning from someone else, then it is well worth the read. The two following book recommendations are a wonderful start because they each include several diva stories: *The Soulful Divas* by David Nathan (Billboard Books), and *Shout, Sister, Shout:*

> "I was sixteen, living in Consort, Alberta, in the middle of nowhere, and by the magic of God, I heard Kate Bush on the radio and just about died.
>
> *k.d. lang*

Ten Girl Singers Who Shaped a Century by Roxane Orgill (Margaret K. McElderry Books).

Magazines

While you're at the library or bookstore, check out the magazine section. There are several periodicals dedicated to the working singer and musician, and they can help to give you a broader view of the business and keep you current. *Singer, Gig,* and *OnStage* magazines are my favorites. They always include interviews with working professionals, in which they are asked interesting questions about their road to the top, practice schedules, and personal philosophy, as well as articles on vocal health and technique. *Rolling Stone* and *Spin* are also helpful and fun reads for the musically minded. Treat yourself to at least one subscription.

The Newsstand

Take regular trips to the newsstand, especially on Friday, as that day's edition is more likely to have all the live music entertainment information. Your local paper can give you a good feel for what's happening around town, as far as where to find live entertainment, what kinds of bands and styles of music are popular in your area, and a general sense of the job market. For instance, if you see an abundance of country-and-folk music entertainment advertised, it may be a clue to gear your repertoire in that direction. Or you may notice a musical void in your area that needs to be filled—by you.

Even more helpful are the free entertainment rag magazines that are often left lying around a newsstand. Many times they have a classified section just for singers and musicians, and that is where you'll find audition announcements and people looking for other singers and musicians to jam with. I found my current band this way, and I've been happily working with them for nine years. Peruse any local papers you can find for yet another way to immerse yourself into your local music scene.

School/College Campuses

Regardless of whether you're in school or not, take advantage of bulletin boards located in campus common areas. Students often use them as free classifieds to find people with similar musical tastes and objectives. Check them periodically to see if anything looks appealing. In general, this age group is much more willing to get together simply for the fun of making music, and this sort of informal jam session is a great, low-pressure way to get accustomed to working with other musicians. I've seen many bands form this way, and even if it goes no farther than a weekly jam session, you'll still have gained some valuable experience. I always recommend to my voice students who are working their way through college to get busy practicing with a band. College towns always have need for live entertainment, and performing beats a waitress job any day.

Surrounding Areas

PRACTICAL GEM
If you're in a small town, you may need to expand your playing field by doing some traveling to neighboring towns or to the closest city to find job opportunities.

By taking some field trips beyond your immediate surroundings, you'll start to get a more realistic view of the market, and you'll discover if a commute is in your future. Due to a family situation, I once moved to a tiny town in North Carolina for nine months. At first it appeared to be a dead end for my singing career—unless I was quick to learn an extensive bluegrass repertoire. But I decided to take some field trips anyway, and one was to a nearby college town where I put up a notice in the student union. A guitar player whose act involved him playing along with prerecorded bass and drum tracks soon responded. He already had a gig lined up, but he was short a vocalist, so we set up a few rehearsals and shortly thereafter, I was back in business. Four evenings a week I drove an hour each way, up and down a mountain, to a ski resort town where we performed at a popular restaurant.

The Karaoke Store

The last field trip is to the karaoke store to find a karaoke CD with which to begin practicing. There are literally thousands of CDs available, ranging from old standards to the most current Top-Forty hits. They are highly effective for practicing the songs you have in mind for your repertoire before you get with an actual accompanist or band, as they provide the music and background vocal tracks without the lead voice. This enables you to clearly hear your strengths and weaknesses, because you alone are carrying the melody. In other words, Whitney Houston isn't singing along with you anymore to nail those high notes for you when you don't quite reach them.

With this in mind, make sure you don't start with a karaoke CD that is too challenging. Pick a singer that has a similar range and style (one that you've been able to easily sing along with on the radio) so you can ease into the karaoke experience. Even with a perfect match, I'll caution you that this can be a rather rude awakening. Be patient, keep your sense of humor, and realize that making big glaring mistakes is the only way you're going to be able to hear and accurately fix them, as I'll explain in further detail in chapter 5.

Additional Karaoke Sources

If you don't have a karaoke store nearby, you can go to a shop online to find what you're looking for. A few of the bigger resources on the Web are East Coast Karaoke (*www.eastcoastkaraoke.com*), Karaoke Now (*www.karaokenow.com*), and Shop Karaoke (*www.shopkaraoke.com*). I also like the quality of Karaoke Bay (*www.karaokebay.com*) and Singing Machine (*www.singingmachine.com*).

PRACTICAL GEM
If you don't have a specific song in mind, places like Target and Wal-Mart usually have a small selection of reasonably priced karaoke compilation CDs.

The Value of a Thank-You Note

I have a feeling that on your travels throughout your local music scene, you are going to meet people who are especially helpful and generous in sharing information with you. I may be biased, but in general, music people are very cool. In my experience, the musician stereotype of the irresponsible, drinking, smoking, drugging loner is a huge misconception, and the majority of professional musicians and singers are amazing souls.

> "With the power of conviction, there is no sacrifice.
>
> *Pat Benatar*

So when you encounter that wonderful salesperson at the music store who patiently answers all your questions and the kind musician at a live music venue who takes time on his break to talk to you, show your appreciation the diva way.

GOLDEN RULE
Send a thank-you note via e-mail or snail mail to all those magnanimous folks who help you along the way.

The gesture, when done well, is always a pleasant surprise to the recipient and works for you on so many levels (see appendix A). First, there is the immediate sense of being appreciated the person will feel when you tell her exactly how she helped you—that's worth the price of a stamp by itself. When you include the details of where you met, you'll make the association complete, thus becoming more memorable in the person's mind. And finally, the overall effect is that you'll be remembered in a positive light, which promotes good relations and referrals for the future. Take a few moments to show your gratitude. You'll soon discover that little things make a big difference.

"Ongoing" Is the Key Word

These field trips aren't a one-shot deal, and they're not something you should do every once in a while, when the mood strikes you. No, if you want to make real progress, the key word here is "ongoing." You need to refer to the list below and choose at least one field trip to go on every week, and once you've gone on all nine, start over. Once again, let me remind you that it's the baby steps you take every day with your practice, and now every week with a field trip, that will get you to that diva promised land. Now, let me hear an amen!

Ongoing Field Trips

* ❊ Live music venues
* ❊ Video store
* ❊ Music store
* ❊ Online music communities and resources
* ❊ Newsstand
* ❊ Karaoke store
* ❊ Library or bookstore
* ❊ Surrounding towns and cities
* ❊ School/college campuses

Find the Will for a Way

I'm guessing that some of you are going to have to step out of your comfort zone to do what is crucial for your diva training. If certain field trips seem more intimidating, build up your confidence with the successful completion of others before attempting them. For example, maybe reading an inspiring diva biography will be just the thing to fire you up to go to the music store and ask some questions. Or perhaps first finding a supportive online music community will give you the bravado to visit a nearby college campus. And you can always turn a field trip into a social occasion to make it more palatable. Make an evening out of your field trips to live music venues or the closest city by inviting a special someone, a group of friends, or co-workers to join you. Try keeping your emotional attachment to the outcome at bay by taking an analytical approach to your field trips. Think of yourself as a scholar doing research and collecting data for a very important project. Do whatever it takes, and I promise that soon your momentum will build into an unstoppable force.

What Your Choices Reveal

As would any self-respecting teacher at the completion of a school field trip, I need to test you to make sure you were paying attention. So often the answers to our most burning questions are right in front of our faces, and if we don't pay attention, we miss the signs that are showing us exactly the way to proceed. I'm a firm believer that there are no coincidences—that the book we happen upon in the library or the person we run into at the music store is in some way connecting the dots to a larger picture. So as you complete each field trip, answer the corresponding question below to reveal clues that will further define your goal in your local music market.

The No-Coincidences Questionnaire

❅ **Live music venue:** Where did you go, who was performing, and is it a place where you could see yourself performing?

❅ **Video/DVD store:** What live-in-concert video did you rent, and what were the three main ideas you took away from watching it?

✳ **Music store:** Whom did you meet, and did you glean any help-ful information? (Even if it was only the salesperson, write it down.)

✳ **Online music community or resource:** Where did you land in cyberspace, and what about the site did you find most beneficial at this stage?

✳ **Library or bookstore:** What diva biography did you read, and why did it appeal to you?

✳ **Newsstand:** After reading several local newspapers, what did you find pertaining to the music scene in your area? What are your thoughts?

✳ **School/college campuses:** What, if any, notices or flyers caught your eye?

✳ **Surrounding areas:** Where did you visit, and did you gather any pertinent information?

✳ **Karaoke store**: What CD did you buy and why?

To Sum It Up

The purpose of this chapter is twofold. First, I have shown you how to immerse yourself into your local music scene with a regular schedule of field trips in order to gather information, to start feel-ing a sense of community, and to create a network by meeting peo-ple in your chosen field. Secondly, I've provided many resources such as books and Web sites so that you can get a better understand-ing of the music business in general. Surrounding yourself either directly or indirectly with talented, like-minded people is going to make you rise to the occasion and stir you to action. Be bold, woman! The most incredible things happen when you start setting your dream in motion.

A DIVA NEXT DOOR SAYS

Stay onstage with the band and play a percussion instrument even when you aren't singing. It looks better to see the band as a whole on the stage, and you'll avoid other hazards as well. I was in the habit of using the ladies' room when one of the other band members was singing a song, rather than waiting until the band was on break. One night I took longer than usual because on my way back from the bathroom, I got cornered by some bar patrons wanting to chat. When I realized that the band was waiting for me to start a song, I ran to get back to the stage, and my strapless dress slipped down below my waist. Talk about learning a lesson the hard way! –Janet

CHAPTER 4

Let's Get Physical

YOUR BODY IS YOUR INSTRUMENT

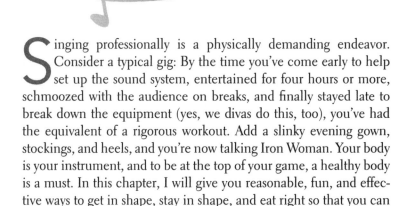

S inging professionally is a physically demanding endeavor. Consider a typical gig: By the time you've come early to help set up the sound system, entertained for four hours or more, schmoozed with the audience on breaks, and finally stayed late to break down the equipment (yes, we divas do this, too), you've had the equivalent of a rigorous workout. Add a slinky evening gown, stockings, and heels, and you're now talking Iron Woman. Your body is your instrument, and to be at the top of your game, a healthy body is a must. In this chapter, I will give you reasonable, fun, and effective ways to get in shape, stay in shape, and eat right so that you can always sing, feel, and look like a diva.

Exercise

An exercise program that includes aerobic activities combined with weight training three times a week is essential for your basic health.

Now, if you're already active in swimming (excellent for building stamina, fitness, and breath control), jogging, kickboxing, inline skating, yoga (which centers around the same breathing technique as singing), organized sports, or whatever, you know how advantageous physical activity is to singing. But if you're anything like I was, you're starting to squirm just thinking about this latest development. For years I jumped on every fad fitness and diet plan bandwagon, only to quit once the novelty wore off. The desire to make my body look a certain way never proved to be motivation enough for me to stick to anything.

The Big Payoff

My sporadic exercise and dieting changed dramatically, however, when I started performing. Why? Because of the big payoff. By consistently exercising and eating right, I was getting closer to phrasing a verse like Nancy Wilson and holding out a note like Barbra Streisand without my face turning bright red and beads of sweat forming on my brow. And well, I did start to notice that I was looking pretty damn good in those evening gowns.

So as you read this chapter and hopefully start making healthier choices, stay focused on your big payoff. I find that if, while exercising, I listen on headphones to songs I want to add to my repertoire and visualize myself performing them, I can stay highly motivated. A picture of your favorite diva on the refrigerator door can also help tremendously. Every time I walk past my photo of Madonna, I see a forty-something-year-old woman with two children, singing and looking better than ever, and I find it much easier to pass up the cookies for a piece of fruit and get fired up to go for my workout.

> "Somebody wrote, "How can she rock in a Versace gown?" Well, easy . . . let me show you.
> *Madonna*

Walking

If you are starting from zero activity, it's probably a good idea to get a physical before you begin your new exercise program. Once you've been given the go-ahead by a doctor, I highly recommend that you start with walking.

> **PRACTICAL GEM**
> *Walking is by far the most convenient and inexpensive exercise.*

When you exercise by walking, you can literally step out your front door and be on your way, which makes you much more likely to stick with a regimen. And walking is easy to work into your daily routine. I'll put in a twenty-minute walk around the mall before I start any serious shopping. Or I'll walk around the parking lot for a half an hour while my daughter is taking her dance lesson. If you're working or going to school all day, you can use half of your lunch hour to get in your thirty minutes. And with no gym membership required, all you need to invest in is a pair of good walking shoes.

Another convenient aspect of walking is that you can easily increase your time and intensity as you build your skill level. Get your upper body in the action by keeping good posture, contracting your stomach muscles, bending your arms at the elbows, and carrying some handheld weights while you walk. There are also the stress-relief benefits. I make an effort to walk while focusing on my deep breathing for an hour a few times a week. For me, there's nothing like it for mind-clearing meditation.

A Complete Fitness Program

From what I can gather from talking to others who regularly work out, there are two camps: those who love the aerobic exercise but would rather enter a bikini contest than do the weight training, and those who think weight training is fun, but find any excuse to get out of doing their aerobics each week. I think the resistance to a complete fitness program in both camps boils down to the unrealistic time demands it seems to require, and perhaps a sense of being overwhelmed. Well, whether you're in the first camp, second camp, or no camp at all, hold on to your sports bra, because I've got the program for you.

The Ultimate Diva Workout

I asked personal trainer and founder of "The No Excuse Workout," Carmela Tafoya, to consider the specific needs of a professional vocalist and design the Ultimate Diva Workout. Having trained over five thousand people, including opera and rock singers, as well as Emily Saliers of the Indigo Girls, I knew she was the perfect person for the job. I told her that we divas need stamina to give three- to five-hour, high-energy performances, and that we need strong lungs for singing. I also mentioned that we need muscle power to lift and carry equipment for setup and breakdown. And finally, I told her we are busy gals who don't want to spend two hours in the gym every day. Oh, yeah, I also mentioned we want to look hot!

Carmela came through with this tailor-made, forty-minute, at-home program. For the cardio work, she is a big proponent of short periods (twenty to thirty minutes) of interval training (slowing and speeding the heart rate at some sort of interval) to build stamina. For the weight training, she has concluded that when the exercises are done with no rest in between, only one set of each is necessary to strengthen every muscle group and produce an overall fit appearance. She is adamant that weight training equals weight loss, and with a mere fifteen minutes, two or three times a week, even this first camp exerciser can comply. She recommends doing the cardio work immediately following the weight training three times a week for optimum results.

Weight Training: Fifteen Minutes, Two to Three Times a Week

Begin with a five-minute warm-up by marching in place. Using three- to eight-pound weights, do one set of ten to twelve repetitions of each exercise below with no rest in between. A good rule to determine the correct amount of weight to start with for each muscle group is to use the weight that makes the last two repetitions a real challenge—in other words, you want to feel the burn. Always use slow, controlled movements, exhale on the exertion, and focus on contracting the muscle being used. If you've never lifted free weights, it will be necessary to either book a session with a qualified personal trainer to learn proper form and technique, or invest in an instructional video. The *Shaping Up with Weights for Dummies* video is a good one for learning the basics.

NINE MAJOR MUSCLE GROUP EXERCISES

* ❈ Crunches (abs)
* ❈ Lunges (quads, glutes, hamstrings)
* ❈ Squats (quads, glutes, hamstrings)
* ❈ Toe raises (calves)
* ❈ Lying-flat presses (pecs)
* ❈ Rows (lats)
* ❈ Overhead presses (delts)
* ❈ Curls (biceps)
* ❈ Kickbacks (triceps)

Interval Cardio Work: Twenty to Thirty Minutes, Three Times a Week

Following the weight training, stretch for five minutes. Walk brusquely for one minute and then jog for three minutes alternately. Stay mindful of your breathing for the duration of the cardio exercise. If you are starting from zero activity, begin with eight-minute intervals of twenty seconds of jogging and ten seconds of standing still, and build up to twenty minutes in three-minute increments.

Program Burnout

The beauty of a complete fitness program is that it gives you a regi-
mented schedule and the direction to get you on course, or back on
course, whatever the case may be. The danger of any one program,
however, is that it may become monotonous, and you will then quit
altogether. (I am willing to bet you have invested in at least one
piece of exercise equipment or video that
now sits in the corner gathering dust.) So
in order to avoid program burnout and
maintain an active lifestyle, I recommend that you regularly allow yourself to
skip a workout and take a "better than
nothing" day.

> They love me, they hate
> me, but they all say,
> "Shit, she looks good!"
> *Bette Midler*

"Better than Nothing" Day

A "better than nothing" day means that rather than beat yourself up
on the days when you can't find the motivation to board the tread-
mill or lift another dumbbell, you find a physical activity that sounds
interesting, or fun, or feasible in your current state of mind, and do
it. Sometimes I'll clean the house from top to bottom instead of
working out, because it seems the lesser of two evils that day and,
hey, it's "better than nothing." On the days I can't resist the lure of
that seductive couple—the couch and the TV—during the com-
mercials, I'll get up and do jumping jacks, push-ups, or sit-ups. Or
you can try my trick of "power window-shopping" by walking at a
good clip around the mall for twenty or thirty minutes. Take a
leisurely bike ride, find a beautiful park to explore on foot, do some
gardening. Or if these activities are too boring for your taste, how
about taking a strip aerobics class? (I'm going to look into this
myself.) Do anything—even if it isn't necessarily productive, organized, or disciplined—other than return to total inactivity. By taking
"better than nothing" days, you'll soon be in the habit of including
some physical activity every day, and you'll never again have to start
a program from ground zero.

"Better than Nothing" Day Activities

* ❅ Dance
* ❅ Do yardwork
* ❅ Play putt-putt golf
* ❅ Walk or play fetch with the dog
* ❅ Clean the house
* ❅ Go bowling
* ❅ Wash the car
* ❅ Frolic in the pool
* ❅ Power window-shop
* ❅ Go roller-skating or bike riding
* ❅ Do TV commercial exercises

"Diet" Is a Four-Letter Word

As far as the diet goes, well, here's the skinny on the bottom line: We all know that there's no need here for some new diet plan. The magic formula for losing and maintaining a healthy weight is common knowledge: Eat five small meals a day that include a variety of fresh fruits, vegetables, nuts, beans, legumes, and lean meats, and go easy on the bad fats and carbs (processed foods and/or foods not from the earth). With that said, I also know that it isn't easy. I'm almost as passionate about food as I am about singing. In fact, there's nothing I enjoy more than combining the two by stopping for a 1:00 A.M. breakfast at an all-night diner with the band to celebrate a successful gig. However, evening gowns aren't cheap. And when even the best control-top pantyhose can't keep me from looking like a sausage in a too-tight casing, I don't say that four-letter word "diet." I say, "It's time to bake some cookies!" (This is reverse psychology at its best.)

"Goodbye, Control-Top!"

Huh? That's right—it's time to head to the grocery store and fill my cart with chocolate chips, oranges, walnuts, and dried cranberries to make "Diva Biscotti." Let me explain. Biscotti are low-fat Italian cookies, the name of which literally means "baked twice." I discovered these little treasures at my favorite bookstore cafe when I was trying to get back to my fighting weight and wanted a light snack. They really hit my finicky sweet spot, and I decided to bake some myself to have on hand during my Häagen-Dazs hiatus.

After trying out a few recipes, experimenting with different ingredients, making some nutritious additions, and having family, friends, and voice students taste test, I came up with "Diva Biscotti." I also dropped a few pounds in the process. Instead of denying myself a sweet for breakfast or with my afternoon coffee or tea, I indulged in one or two cookies and was able to stick to my program long enough to say, "Goodbye, control-top!"

The Baking Ritual

The activity starts with a ritual: Before you begin baking, you should set the mood by putting on some great diva music.

BAKING MUSIC

* Aretha Franklin, *Aretha's Best*
* Celine Dion, *Falling into You*
* Destiny's Child, *Survivor*
* The Dixie Chicks, *FLY*
* Ella Fitzgerald, *Live in Berlin*
* Jessica Andrews, *Now*
* Madonna, *Music*
* Martina McBride, *Evolution*
* No Doubt, *Rock Steady*
* Peggy Lee, *The Best of Miss Peggy Lee*
* Sheryl Crow, *Tuesday Night Music Club*

Next, assemble ingredients, mix, bake, and dance. No, really, it makes perfect sense. There are approximately fifty minutes of baking time with this recipe, so you have a perfect window of opportunity to jump-start your program. Just picture dancing around the house to your favorite diva CD while mouthwatering aromas waft from the oven. Could there be a more enjoyable calorie-burning workout? (Dancing for just twenty minutes burns one hundred calories.) And of course, you'll end the ritual by guiltlessly eating the fruits of your labor. Mmmmm, divalicious!

TASTY TIDBIT: DIVA BISCOTTI

* 1 cup whole wheat flour
* ⅔ cup white flour
* ½ cup sugar
* ¼ teaspoon salt
* ¼ teaspoon orange extract
* 2 tablespoons fresh orange juice
* 1 teaspoon baking soda
* 2 large eggs
* 1 teaspoon vanilla extract
* grated peel of ⅔ medium orange
* 1 cup semisweet chocolate chips
* 1 cup chopped walnuts
* 1 cup chopped dried cherries or cranberries

Preheat oven to 300°. Combine flour, baking soda, and salt in a small bowl, and mix with a whisk. In a medium bowl, whisk eggs, sugar, vanilla extract, orange extract, and peel. Mix in orange juice. Using a rubber spatula, stir in flour mixture until just combined. Stir in chocolate chips, fruit, and nuts. Batter will be thick and sticky. Scrape batter onto a foil-lined baking sheet, dividing it into two long, skinny loaves, about 14 inches long and 2 to 2½ inches wide. Even up the edges with a spatula. Bake on the middle rack at 300° for 35 minutes or until firm and springy. Let cool 10 minutes on pan. Leave oven turned on.

Use both hands to remove each loaf onto a cutting board, and slice with a serrated knife into ½-inch slices. Lay slices back on the baking sheet, and bake again for 12 minutes. Turn them over and bake for an additional 12 minutes.

> *Cool completely before stacking in an airtight container. They will last several weeks. Makes about 45 small cookies.*

Mom Knew Best

Alas, a diva cannot live on biscotti alone, so I'll also share a few other recipes I've inherited from my mom, who I daresay is one of the original health-food nuts. Back when I was a kid, my very proper, southern-bred mother would no more have served a meal without every major food group represented than she would have gone streaking through our neighborhood wearing nothing but an Easter bonnet. I remember once asking if I could have white bread instead of whole wheat in my lunch box like all the other kids at school, and you'd have thought I'd asked for marijuana-laced brownies. I heard her use the term "healthy, well-balanced meal" so often, that for years I thought it was one really long obnoxious word. But as frustrating as it was as a child to never be able to try the stuff they advertised during Saturday morning cartoons or to eat fast food, I know now that mom knew best.

This soup was one of her staples. She would make a huge pot for dinner at least once a month, and freeze any leftovers for a quick and easy weekend lunch (her idea of "fast food"). I've found this to be the perfect, light pre-gig or anytime meal.

TASTY TIDBIT: MAMA'S VEGGIE BEEF SOUP
* ✳ *1 lb. lean ground beef (round or sirloin)*
* ✳ *1 teaspoon olive oil*
* ✳ *1 cup onion, chopped*
* ✳ *1 large potato, peeled and cubed*
* ✳ *2 celery stalks, chopped*
* ✳ *2 to 3 cloves garlic, minced*
* ✳ *1 15-oz. can each of stewed tomatoes and low salt chicken broth*
* ✳ *1 cube of chicken bouillon*

❄ *2 cups water*
❄ *1 teaspoon each salt and pepper*
❄ *½ of a 16-oz. bag frozen mixed vegetables (corn, carrots, green peas, lima beans, and green beans)*
❄ *1 teaspoon dried basil*
❄ *(optional) 1 cup of any fresh vegetables you happen to have on hand, like yellow squash, tomato, cabbage, or zucchini.*

On the stove in a large pot, brown the ground beef with onions, celery, garlic, olive oil, and salt and pepper. Add chicken broth, water, stewed tomatoes, and bouillon cube, and bring to a boil. Add the potatoes, frozen mixed vegetables, and cup of optional fresh vegetables, and turn down heat to simmer for 30 minutes. Finally, season with basil and salt and pepper to taste.

Extra Good Luck

This next recipe is inspired by a dish called "Hoppin' John." Without fail, my mom makes this on New Year's Day, not only because it is a southern tradition that is supposed to bring good luck for the coming year, but also because it is so delicious. I've added more vegetables and made some changes to save time, calories, and one little piggy—the original recipe calls for a ham hock. I also make it a lot more often than once a year for the extra good luck it always provides. Besides giving lots of energy, this dish has the spiciness that never fails to put me in fine singing voice.

TASTY TIDBIT: LUCKY BEANS AND RICE
❄ *1 20-oz. can black-eyed peas, black beans, or red beans, drained*
❄ *1 or so tablespoons olive oil*
❄ *2 celery stalks, chopped*
❄ *1 small red or green bell pepper, chopped*
❄ *1 medium onion, chopped*

❋ 2 garlic cloves, minced
❋ 1 bay leaf
❋ ½ fresh jalapeno, seeds removed, chopped
❋ 1½ teaspoons salt
❋ white, wild, yellow, or brown rice

On the stove in a large skillet, sauté celery, onions, garlic, pepper, and jalapeno in olive oil until soft. Turn down heat to low, and mix in the beans, bay leaf, and salt. Cover and simmer while preparing rice. In a separate pot, prepare the rice according to package directions. To serve, spoon the bean mixture over rice, and garnish with hot sauce or chunky salsa.

Eating Pasta Isn't a Sin

I don't care how many doctors go on about the sin of eating carbs, I'll never be convinced that eating a bowl of pasta smothered in my mom's divine sauce isn't one of life's greatest and most necessary pleasures. Again, this dish is full of healthy stuff and will give you the energy to get through even the longest gig.

TASTY TIDBIT: PASTA DIVINE
❋ 1 lb. hot turkey sausage
❋ 2–3 garlic cloves, minced
❋ 2 teaspoons olive oil
❋ 1 small onion, chopped (sweet Vidalia is best)
❋ 4 cups marinara sauce (homemade or store-bought—I use Ragú)
❋ 1 3-oz. bag sun-dried tomatoes, chopped
❋ ¼ teaspoon each dried basil, oregano, and thyme
❋ 1 bay leaf
❋ ¾ cup fresh or frozen cut leaf spinach
❋ dash of crushed red peppers
❋ 1 lb. any wide noodle pasta

Remove sausage from casing, and separate as you brown with olive oil, garlic, and onion in a large pot on medium high heat. Add remaining ingredients and reduce heat. Allow to simmer while preparing pasta according to package directions. To serve, spoon sauce over pasta, and sprinkle with fresh grated Parmesan cheese.

Girls Just Wanna Have Fun

As is demonstrated by my Diva Biscotti approach to starting a weight-loss program, I'm always searching for the most enjoyable way to break my bad habits or change an unhealthy pattern. And when it comes to eating a balanced diet, counting calories, weighing portions, or dialing a meal don't fit the bill. Awhile back, I read about a novel approach for remembering to eat the five recommended servings of fruits and vegetables a day. I thought it sounded like a fun way to motivate my daughter to make healthy choices even when I wasn't around to guide her. Well, it was such a huge success that I ended up joining in the fun.

The Five-a-Day Bracelet Plan

For this plan, you need five beaded stretch bracelets in five different colors that can be easily removed. We got some brightly colored ones at a dollar store, but you can go to a bead shop and get crafty, or feel free to splurge on something more fancy. You start out in the morning with all five bracelets on one wrist, and as you eat a fruit or vegetable serving (½ cup), you move a bracelet to the other wrist. By the end of the day, all your bracelets should be on the opposite wrist. The five different colors will serve to remind you to choose a variety of fruits and vegetables. I can't tell you how many times I go to the kitchen intending to eat something less than nutritious, and seeing that I still have three bracelets to move for the day, go for the good stuff instead. It is then far less likely that after having eaten a big juicy apple, I'll proceed to eat the piece of chocolate cake that I'd initially craved. It really works, and how can a weight-loss tool that begins with buying jewelry go wrong?

TASTY TIDBIT
Buy an apple corer. This nifty device cuts apples and other small, round fruits into perfect wedges, making a fruit serving both convenient and appetizing—and you will eat more fruit as a result.

The Wee Small Hours

So let's assume that all is going as planned. You're exercising regularly and making nutritious food choices—and then you begin the dream job. Wonderful, except I need to warn you about a possible occupational hazard that even the most health-conscious performers struggle to avoid. Any performer will tell you that the hardest time to resist pigging out is late at night or early in the morning, after you've expended lots of calories on a gig and most likely haven't eaten since dinner. I try to avoid this, and I recommend you do, too, by bringing an energy bar to your gigs, but I don't always have the foresight. Rather than fall into the drive-thru line, have the ingredients for a satisfying Cool Down Smoothie on hand at home. It will relieve your grumbling stomach, soothe your parched throat, and you can move two bracelets because of the two fruit servings it includes—it's all good.

TASTY TIDBIT: COOL DOWN SMOOTHIE
❊ *½ cup each frozen strawberries and blueberries*
❊ *1 6-oz. container low-fat vanilla yogurt*
❊ *⅓ cup vanilla soy milk*

Mix all ingredients in a blender until smooth.

Looking the Part

It bears mentioning here that by leading a healthy lifestyle, you're also helping yourself to look the part, which, right or wrong, is no small advantage. Early in my career, I performed every weekend at a supper club. We had been there about a month when a regular approached the stage, and I overheard him tell the bandleader that the shorter my skirt, the better I sounded. Of course, my feminist sensibilities were offended. But once I got over that, I gained important insight from his comment: Essentially, you are selling a product—your talent. The more attractive the packaging, the more people are going to buy it.

To Sum It Up

Regular exercise and a balanced diet are going to have an almost immediate effect on your ability as a singer in the physical sense. As I said in chapter 2, proper breathing is the source from which every beautiful note is sung, and with the recommended cardio work, you'll have the necessary lung capacity to create vocal masterpieces. Combined with the recommended weight training, you'll have the stamina and power for a dynamic performance and the demands of your job. But perhaps even more importantly, getting healthy has profound psychological effects. There is simply no denying the mind/body connection, and by treating your body with reverence, you are sending the message to your mind that you are worthy. You'll then have the much needed confidence (which I'll venture to say is 99 percent of a great performance) to walk into an audition, and ulti-mately a gig, feeling beautiful inside and out and ready to conquer the stage.

A DIVA NEXT DOOR SAYS

I had always been what most would call "big-boned," "pleasantly plump," or "full-figured." It never bothered me that I didn't look like the models in the fashion magazines because I have always been considered attractive by my husband, as well as in the Latin community where I usually perform with a salsa band. But there came a point when I started feeling tired all the time, so I went for a long overdue physical. The doctor told me that my blood pressure and cholesterol were too high and that I immediately needed to change my diet, start exercising, and lose some weight. Determined not to rely on medicine for my well-being, I followed his diet and exercise recommendations. In addition to looking and feeling ten years younger, I was pleasantly surprised to find that it was much easier and more enjoyable to sing. People told me over and over how I had never sounded better, and I had to agree. If I had known how even twenty extra pounds could negatively affect my general health, energy level, and singing voice, I think I would have cut back on the fried plantains and flan a lot sooner. –Carmen

The Bridge

Making the Transition from Hobbyist to Professional

The Bridge

Reveal the beauty that's been hidden deep inside.
Gonna open up my wings, it's my time to fly.

When the bridge of a song is well written, it provides a seamless yet highly effective departure from the verse allowing for a smooth flow into the climactic chorus. In phase 2, I've embraced this ideal to prepare you for a graceful transition from hobbyist to professional. I shine the light on the nitty-gritty details that separate the women from the divas.

Everything from how to best memorize a song, to conquering stage fright and dealing with hecklers, to the rules of etiquette is covered. I also list and give budget advice for all the necessary purchases, like a quality vocal microphone, a stunning diva wardrobe, and a killer résumé.

Phase 2 can be a period of huge growth and fulfillment if you are willing to do the work and take the risks that it requires. You will need to further commit yourself by giving more time, energy, and money to the process, but take my word, the rewards are priceless.

CHAPTER 5

Get Ready

FINE-TUNING YOUR ACT

A t this point, you should be much better acquainted with your local music scene. You've been out to see the different bands around town, talked to some people in the biz, and hopefully you're starting to get a feel for how you would like to fit into the picture. You are now ready to build your repertoire, fine-tune your practice, and organize a songbook in order to be thoroughly prepared for singing in public.

> Instead of always looking at the past, I put myself ahead twenty years and try to look at what I need to do now in order to get there then.
>
> *Diana Ross*

Repertoire

When you're choosing songs for your repertoire, each selection is extremely important. You are compiling a song list that, depending on its content, could mean the difference between getting and keeping a job or not. It's about knowing who your audience is going to be. For example, if your goal is to sing in a country-and-western band, you had better have a Patsy Cline classic like "Crazy" on your list. Or if you'd like to see yourself in a wedding or party band, a line dance song like the "Electric Slide" or "Hot, Hot, Hot" is mandatory. The band you are auditioning for will expect it, and so will its audience.

A One-Woman Show

As you build your repertoire, aim for between twenty-five and thirty selections, and approach it as if you are putting together a one-woman show. You are going to want a great opening number and a great closer with a dynamic and danceable selection of songs in between. Pull out your field-trip notes, and look at the songs that got people fired up or had them filing onto the dance floor. I'm not suggesting that you can't choose songs that you especially love or do particularly well, but keep in mind this fact that years of experience has revealed to me.

TRICK OF THE TRADE
Song choice is key to a favorable audience response.

As far as the general audience is concerned, a good singer is one who can perform their song requests. This may seem a bit simplistic, and even a little offensive, considering you've put in countless hours of hard work to become a quality vocalist. Well, no offense intended, but I've seen one too many audiences turn on a great, wonderfully talented band when they couldn't produce a few of their favorites.

The Polish Club Debacle

A perfect example is the time our band got booked at the Polish Club in town. The gig was on a weeknight and didn't interfere with our steady house gig at the poo-poo-la-la club across the bridge, so we agreed to do it. We felt confident that as long as we learned a few polkas to play during the evening (the piano player also played accordion), the gig would be a breeze, and we'd be a big hit. It didn't quite turn out that way.

Who knew that these Polish people loved Italian music? After playing the only three Italian numbers we knew, the requests kept coming in for more, and we could feel the enthusiasm level falling. Time to bring out the big guns. The piano player strapped on the fifty-pound accordion to play a polka, and the dance crowd dwindled to about four couples within seconds! The breeze gig turned out to be a disaster, and all because we didn't have the right repertoire for the audience.

The Six Steps to Mastering a Song

There are six steps that are necessary to truly master a song and get it performance-ready:

* ❊ Study a great singer's rendition
* ❊ Feel the rhythm with your shaker
* ❊ Memorize the lyrics
* ❊ Work through the kinks
* ❊ Sing with the karaoke music
* ❊ Give it a soul injection

> It's not about sitting with your butt on the sofa and going, "I wanna be a star." No way. You've got to know how to bake the bread before eating it and there's just so much you need to know, and I knew I had to learn it.
>
> *Lara Fabian*

Study the Greats

Once you've chosen a song, find a recording done by a great singer and learn directly from a master how to phrase and deliver the song. Listen carefully, repeatedly, and visualize yourself absorbing the greatness—like musical osmosis. Then sing along, mimicking every nuance. I would recommend you lean toward the female greats rather than the male, only because the male renditions are less likely to be in a comfortable key for a female voice. There is much to learn from my men Frank, Stevie, James, Sting, Luther, and Clay, but for these initial purposes, stick with the female greats.

PRACTICAL GEM

Go to an online music store to purchase and download single songs instead of buying the entire CD. I use iTunes (apple.com/itunes/store) *and Real One Rhapsody* (Real.com), *but dozens of new online music stores are introduced every day.*

Some will argue that a singer doesn't develop her own personal style if she is always copying others, but I have found this to be completely untrue. Aspiring painters are encouraged to study Picasso, Van Gogh, and Rembrandt, and though these masters may influence their early work, in time, the painter's own artistic expression emerges. This is the case for singers as well. Several years ago, for example, I learned the jazz standard "Lullaby of Birdland" by listening to a recording done by the incomparable Sarah Vaughn. My rendition today sounds nothing like hers, as it has evolved with me over time, and that has been the case for every song I've ever learned in this manner.

Feel the Rhythm

Remember that shaker you bought at the music store? Get it out now, and try to keep simple, steady time with the recording. Feeling the rhythm of the music will help you phrase the song appropriately. For instance, a swing, a bossa nova, and a disco beat are distinctly different. The other members of the band will know this, and you should, too. So listen carefully, and keep that shaker going. With practice, you'll begin to not only hear the words and the melody when you are learning a song, but you'll start to feel the song on a rhythmic level.

Many of the most gifted musicians and singers of all time have either started out on or included the drums or some form of percussion in their education because it is the driving force, the heartbeat, of all music. For example, the exquisite Karen Carpenter thought of herself as a drummer first and foremost. There's no question that her strong sense of rhythm had a part in her ability to dig into a song and create the perfect marriage of lyrics and melody every time she sang. Work with your shaker so that you, too, can feel the heartbeat of your songs.

Memorize the Lyrics

It is best if you memorize your lyrics so you'll then have one less element to distract you from delivering the song with complete confidence and feeling. Some people find it easy to memorize lyrics by simply listening to a recording a few times, but others require a little extra effort.

TRICK OF THE TRADE
To best memorize a song, use as many senses as possible.

You've already been listening to and singing along with the recording, and using the shaker to feel the rhythm of the song. To employ even more senses, type the lyrics in bold capital letters on an eight-and-a-half by twelve-inch sheet of paper, and put it in a clear, plastic page protector for safekeeping. This will eventually go in your songbook for a reference on gigs, but for now, use it to read the lyrics as you sing them. You should be able to retain the words to hundreds of songs by going through this process each time. The memorization process may seem like overkill now as you sing in the comfortable surroundings of your own home. But add a brightly lit stage, an audience, and the typical performance jitters, just to name a few variables in live performance, and you'll be very glad you put in the extra time and effort. Andrea Marcovicci—the brilliant cabaret performer who has had an incredible sixteen-year run at New York's Algonquin Hotel and has hundreds of songs in her repertoire—once pointed out to me an additional payoff for memorizing songs: "It's better than ginkgo biloba."

TRICK OF THE TRADE
The quickest way to find lyrics on the Internet is to go on a search engine like Google and type the name of the song in quotation marks followed by the word "lyrics."

Work through the Kinks

Using a metronome set to the tempo of the song to keep you in time, sing the song a capella, only moving forward once you've worked through the problem areas. Practicing the entire song incorrectly over and over will only result in further entrenching the bad habit, making it much more difficult to rectify later. Refer back to chapter 2 if necessary to help you pinpoint the cause of a trouble spot. For instance, don't forget to mark an X on your lyric sheet everywhere you need to take a breath. So often, a weak delivery is simply due to not breathing often enough to support the voice.

Or maybe you keep hitting a brick wall when you go for the big ending that includes the highest note of the song. I've found this to be a common dilemma with my students, and it is usually due to a mental state rather than a physical weakness. They literally psyche themselves right out of nailing the note by telling themselves that there's no way in the world they can possibly do it, and then falling flat because they don't approach the note with confidence. It's the classic self-fulfilling prophecy.

If there are a group of notes you're having trouble singing (e.g., you aren't able to sing each note in tune and/or quickly enough to stay in time), repeatedly sing them very slowly, and then gradually increase the tempo until you reach that of the song. This method of slowing down and gradually speeding up is very effective for working through and fixing a trouble spot.

REAL PROGRESS

The point here is that there are several lessons to be learned in every song you sing, and if you want to make real progress, you must dissect, analyze, and work through each little glitch in practice. It may feel like getting through a song is taking forever, but remember that in the process, you are developing muscle, refining your technique, and raising your skill level, which you can then apply to the next song. You'll get more and more proficient, and in time, mastering a song won't take nearly as long.

> I think it takes obsession, it takes searching for the details, for any artist to be good.
>
> *Barbra Streisand*

VOICE LESSONS

If you find that you still can't figure out or rectify a problem, it may be time, if you haven't already, to sign up for some voice lessons. When there, ask the teacher to work with you on the songs for your repertoire. Sometimes it just takes a month or two of one-on-one instruction to make a major breakthrough. Every teacher has a unique way of communicating the same principles, and it's very possible that with the right teacher, you'll suddenly grasp a concept that has previously eluded you.

Not too long ago, I went for a few refresher lessons with a highly regarded voice coach in Miami, primarily to understand how I could make the notes in my lower range sound more full. In just one lesson, she helped considerably. I sang a rangy song from my repertoire for her that had always felt strained whenever I got to the low notes. When I finished singing, she explained that I simply needed to talk the low notes rather than trying so hard to sing them, and the mystery was solved.

Sing with the Karaoke Music

Singing with the background tracks of your karaoke CD can be the really fun part, as long as you reserve it for after you've completed the prior steps. Prematurely singing to the karaoke music tracks can be downright discouraging, so don't jump the gun. By the time you settle into this step, you should have the lyrics memorized, a strong sense of the rhythm, your breathing pattern established, kinks resolved, and be closely acquainted with the lead vocal melody. Once you've completed these steps, then sing, sing, sing! Close your eyes and channel the talent of the diva you learned from into every note. Summon energy from your whole body to serve the song. If you can sing with this kind of focused mental and physical concentration instead of thinking about household chores, homework, or errands you need to do, you will make speedy progress.

Good Microphone Technique

If you happen to have an actual karaoke machine, take advantage of the microphone. Not only does it help to keep you from straining your voice in practice, but you can start learning how to use it most effectively. You should hold the mic relatively close to your mouth for the soft and lower notes, and pull the mic away from your mouth in accordance with your volume. Two common mistakes made by inexperienced singers is to pull the mic too far away, in which case the voice isn't amplified enough and can't be heard, or to hold the mic too closely, in which case the voice sounds too loud or distorted. Good microphone technique enables you to create some dynamics in a song to present it in the most flattering way, and it will become second nature with a little practice.

A Soul Injection

For a non-diva, this would be the end of the learning process. But I know you're not interested in settling. Therefore, it just isn't enough that you can sing the song to the best of your ability; you need to completely master the song by giving it a soul injection. Giving a song a soul injection means you are always striving to find some personal meaning or significance in the song, and then sincerely communicating those feelings to your audience. This shouldn't be so hard, right? All you have to do is reveal a glimpse of your soul by exposing raw emotions like heartache, infatuation, joy, disappointment, jealousy, love, and anger to a room full of virtual strangers. Ok, so maybe it's a little harder than you thought . . .

FINDING A SOUL SOURCE

First, it requires real courage to subdue your ego and refrain from the need to prove to the audience how well you sing. (So many singers get caught up in the solitary goal of performing vocal gymnastics.) Then you have to constantly search for a source from which to draw your inspiration for each song. For example, if you are singing a song that has a theme that you can relate to from personal experience, use it to resonate with your audience. If, however, the theme of a song you are singing is beyond your years, experience, or current state of mind, you may have to look outside of yourself. Using empathy helps. You can seek to understand the unfamiliar from your friends and family, literature, theater, visual arts, or any number of other places. The greats draw from whatever is in the moment. Everything from a blister on their heels to help emote pain and suffering to an impolite audience member to help emote anger or displeasure are used to sing a song with soul. They know that

> Music is so weird sometimes, so therapeutic and healing. It's almost like it's waiting to be there for you when you need it—just like a good friend with open arms.
>
> *Reba McEntire*

singing a song without giving it a soul injection will result in a flat performance that's about as satisfying as a sugarless, fat-free dessert—I shudder to think.

Organize a Songbook

Repeat this learning process with every song you choose for your repertoire, and organize your plastic-covered lyric sheets alphabetically by title in a large three-ring binder. This binder is your personal songbook, and it needs to accompany you on every audition and gig. Even though you are memorizing the lyrics as you go, after you've been performing for awhile, you could easily have 200 songs or more in your repertoire. So you can see why it's imperative to always keep your songbook on a music stand by your side in the event that you are given a song request that you don't do very often or to use as a temporary crutch for the newer songs in your repertoire.

An Unfortunate Memory Lapse

I had a "funny now, mortifying then" experience involving my songbook while performing at one of my first wedding receptions. I had been asked at the last minute to learn a special ballad for the couple's first dance, and I didn't have ample time to completely memorize the song. I felt confident, however, because I made sure to set up my handy-dandy songbook on the music stand beside me to cheat if necessary.

But when it came time for the first dance, I couldn't find the lyrics to the song. (I later realized that I'd placed them in the front pocket of my songbook for easy access.) I went ahead and sang, and it went along fine until the last verse in which I drew a total blank, so I sort of mumbled/sang, "you and me, we go together like peanut butter and jelly." (I must have watched a lot of *Barnie* with my daughter that week.) Well, bless those newlywed's hearts; they were so wrapped up in each other, they didn't even seem to notice. I have always wondered if they caught it on the wedding video.

Bust a Move

What is your body doing while you're singing your song? That is the question that needs to be answered by watching yourself in the mirror as you practice at home. It is very possible that you are so caught up in singing the song that you forget to move at all, or that you move in a manner that's distracting, like miming every single word of the song. Give this aspect of your performance some serious consideration.

It's not necessary for you to have every moment of the song choreographed like Britney Spears or Jennifer Lopez, but some simple preplanned movements can make all the difference until this aspect of your performance becomes more natural for you. Refer back to the notes you took on your field trips to live music venues and the video store for some ideas. Sometimes using all of your performance space by periodically walking to different areas of the stage or making eye contact with a few people in the audience can be an effective technique, so use your imagination and simulate a live performance at home. It depends on the song, of course, but maybe a shimmy here or a shake there is in order. Or try using your shaker during the instrumental solo section of certain songs to make for a more visually exciting performance. Give it some thought, and then work out some movement for each song in your repertoire in front of the mirror so you'll look as good as you sound.

Classic Songs

Now I'm going to give you a list of songs to include in your repertoire, along with the names of the divas who made them famous. You may balk at some of the selections, thinking that they're outdated, cheesy, foreign, unhip, or all of the above. But even if you're never required to sing a one of them—which I seriously doubt—this list has classic songs that are representative of many different eras, styles, and rhythms. By learning songs that are less familiar and/or more challenging to you, you'll broaden your musical knowledge and enhance your ability to sing songs that are familiar. Not to mention the fact that you're going to delight audiences with your versatility. Picture this scenario: You look out at your audience noting the different age groups, and then you sing a song from each era. Now, that's entertainment!

Top Ten Must-Learn Songs

* ✳ "Girl from Ipanema," as sung by Astrid Gilberto (bossa nova)
* ✳ "Crazy," as sung by Patsy Cline (country ballad)
* ✳ "I Will Survive," as sung by Gloria Gaynor (disco)
* ✳ "Cabaret," as sung by Liza Minelli (Broadway)
* ✳ "My Guy," as sung by The Supremes (Motown)
* ✳ "Hit Me with Your Best Shot," as sung by Pat Benatar (rock)
* ✳ "Night and Day," as sung by Ella Fitzgerald (jazz swing)
* ✳ "Respect," as sung by Aretha Franklin (soul)
* ✳ "Evergreen," as sung by Barbra Streisand (ballad)
* ✳ "Proud Mary," as sung by Tina Turner (rhythm and blues)

Because Practical Matters

As you start to shell out some money for CDs, organizational supplies, etc., you are shifting from singing as a hobby to singing as a profession. So, some financial advice is now in order. Chapter 7 will go into the bulk of a professional vocalist's expenditures, with ways to cut costs, but even at this developmental stage, it is important to start training yourself to think as a businesswoman. I can assure you that the sooner

> If I didn't have some kind of education, then I wouldn't be able to count my money.
>
> *Missy Elliot*

you come to terms with your financial situation, the better. We passionate, creative, artsy-fartsy types sometimes want to stick our heads in the sand when it comes to such practical matters. But it's going to be necessary for you to use both the left and right sides of your brain to be successful.

PRACTICAL GEM

Keep the receipts for all of your diva purchases, as well as a record of your music-related mileage.

By tax time, you might just be one busy bee, and an accountant familiar with the entertainment business can point out all of your deductible expenses. Also, look at your monthly bills, and start to get a realistic figure of what your income needs to be. Keep in mind that if you're going to be a full-time, self-employed vocalist, you'll be responsible for your own health insurance plan and retirement fund.

Stand Tall

Before we go any further on this diva journey, I need to get something off my chest and hopefully instill in you a richly deserved sense of pride. If you haven't noticed, lounge and wedding singers sometimes get a pretty bad rap in the media and are the punch line to many a joke. But let me tell you something, sister. (Can you tell this is a touchy subject?) Some of the most talented singers ever to hit the big time came from this type of background. Because they had to master so many styles of music in their early careers, singing in one or two styles after they got famous was like a stroll in the park.

Pop sensation Gloria Estefan started as a wedding singer in Miami. Shania Twain performed in a Vegas-style variety show in her native Canada before arriving in Nashville and taking the country-music world by storm. And golden-voiced Maureen McGovern played Holiday Inns across the Midwest before she landed a record deal and sang her hit song "There's Got to Be a Morning After." So embrace the challenges of your craft, and stand tall, knowing that you're conquering one of the hardest jobs in show business. (Whew, I feel much better.)

> We're constantly being told what other people think we are, and that's why it's so important to know yourself.
>
> *Sarah McLachlan*

To Sum It Up

In this chapter, I guide you in choosing the songs for your repertoire and then give a meticulous process for mastering each song. As you study and practice and practice some more in obscurity, you may be thinking that this whole diva thing is starting to feel a lot like work. Well, I don't want to sound like your mother (maybe just a wiser big sister), but there aren't any shortcuts here, missy. And come show time, you are going to want to kiss my perfectly pedicured feet in gratitude for not letting you take the easy way out.

A DIVA NEXT DOOR SAYS

Overestimating your ability is just as detrimental as underestimating your ability. Learning humility has truly been one of the most difficult (yet most important) accomplishments for me as an artist. As my personality has always leaned more toward the strong-willed kind, I was never very graceful when it came to taking constructive criticism. I felt that admitting to any shortcomings was like admitting to failure. Therefore, it always took me longer to arrive at a new and better place. Opening up to other singers and listening and studying other accomplished vocalists has been vital in my growth process. When you allow yourself to do this, you are, in essence, not only honoring another's gift, but your own as well. –Robin

CHAPTER 6

Ain't Nothing Like the Real Thing

YOU'RE ON!

You've done enough prep work, and now it's time to jump in with both feet: You must seize every opportunity to sing in front of an audience. This is scary for most people even if it's exactly what they've always dreamed of doing. The fact is, however, that the only way to work out stage fright, performance jitters, and any kinks in your delivery is to get out there and perform time and time again. Refining your repertoire, getting comfortable and effective with using a microphone, and developing your performance style are just a few of the many benefits. In addition, you will have more occasions to meet key people in your music community and to start defining your image.

Search High and Low

Search the entertainment section of your local newspaper and the music store bulletin boards for open mic nights, jam sessions, amateur nights, and karaoke entertainment. Even if you don't have accompaniment, look for situations where it would be appropriate to sing a cappella or, if you have one, with your own karaoke system. Call on the activities directors at nursing homes and assisted living centers in your community to see if they might like some free entertainment. If your neighborhood has a homeowners' association or a clubhouse, offer to do a

> " I will do one of two things: Make it by the skin of my teeth, or die from exhaustion. And I'd rather die of exhaustion than boredom.
>
> *Jo Dee Messina* "

short performance at the next meeting or social gathering. Company picnics, religious services, block parties, or school fundraisers are also great places to get your feet wet. Keep your eyes and ears open for local talent contests at county fairs or shopping malls, or for opportunities to sing the national anthem at sporting events. You may need to get creative here, but I know if you keep an open mind and a brave heart, you'll find a way to get performing experience.

Chick Singer Night

I'll give you a heads-up on another great opportunity to get performance experience. Chick Singer Night (*www.chicksingernight.com*) is a monthly songfest held in nine major cities across the country and is open to female singers of all styles and levels of experience. The way it works is, you send your local director a short bio, a CD demo, and your contact information. Once you've been given a show date, you arrive that afternoon with your charts, run through them with the CSN band, and later that evening give a performance. I've heard nothing but great things from the women who've participated in this.

Sing Backup

Some of the best experience I had as a beginner was singing backup for a singer/songwriter. At the time, she was performing in a coffee-house making very little money and was happy to get free harmony. It was a perfect baby step because I was close to, but not quite, center stage, and there I was able to grow comfortably.

I got that gig because I loved her music, and when I asked if we could get together sometime to jam, one thing led to another. Ask one of your favorite bands around town if you can come to observe a rehearsal. Once you're there, listen for songs that you could enhance with a missing harmony or a little percussion, and then work on perfecting the part. How can they deny you when you offer to make them sound even better for free?

Stage Fright

I'd be remiss if I didn't share some ways of dealing with the fear and insecurity that is unique to performing in public, especially for, but not limited to, the novice. The symptoms of stage fright range from shallow breathing and jitters to a complete inability to focus or function, all of which hinder a singer to

> " Women have to harness their power—it's absolutely true. It's just learning not to take the first no. And if you can't go straight ahead, you go around the corner.
>
> *Cher* "

some degree. Thorough and meticulous preparation is the best prevention, but if you still feel like your nerves are getting the best of you, perhaps one or more of these practices will help.

Positive Visualization and Affirmations

Try using two thought processes that have served me well. They are called positive visualization and affirmations. Prior to an engagement, instead of obsessing over past mistakes or forecasting future disasters, picture yourself, in great detail, having a flawless performance. Do this while you practice, before you go to sleep at night, and first thing when you wake up in the morning.

Also, silence the critic in your head that only has negative things to say about your ability, and replace it with one strong, positive

statement or affirmation. Every time you catch the inner critic saying something like, "I just know you're going to screw up the song,"
or, "Nobody is going to like the way you sing," tell yourself instead
that, "I am a unique and gifted singer." Even if you don't yet believe
your affirmation, making a conscious effort to replace negative
thoughts with positive ones really helps to put you in the "can do"
mind-set that's so critical to success.

Too Much of a Good Thing

As any performer will tell you, a little nervous energy or that "butter-
flies in the stomach" feeling can be productive. Ideally, this boost of
adrenaline can heighten your senses and give you the extra jolt that
is necessary for a performer to cross the great divide between the
stage and the audience and make a real connection. But if you have
the uncontrollable feeling that you're going to jump right out of
your skin, you might need to do a burst of physical activity to
temper the flow. I've done jumping jacks, marched in place, and
hopped up and down while shaking my arms before going on stage.
You might feel silly, but experience has shown me that too much
nervous energy can cause pitch and breathing problems.

Release the Fear with "the Prayer"

Another practice I use to keep stage fright at bay is what I call the
prayer. It basically involves bending your elbows and placing your
palms together in front of your face, much as one might do in prayer.
Close your eyes and while slowly inhaling, press your palms together
as tightly as possible. While slowly exhaling, release the pressure,
and envision all the fear and uncertainty leaving you. Repeat until
you are focused and breathing slowly.

Push Your Own Panic Button

If all else fails and your chest tightens and your breathing becomes
shallow, try pushing your own built-in panic button. With the three

middle fingers of both hands, find the spot located at the bottom center of your breastbone, just above your abs. Breathing deeply, gradually apply pressure until it almost hurts. Continue applying pressure and breathing deeply for two minutes. The ancient art of acupressure is very effective for releasing tension.

Ooze Divaness

As you take these more public steps toward your goal, it's important to be aware of the image you're projecting. You should absolutely ooze divaness in your appearance and your attitude. I go into great detail regarding appearance in the next chapter, but suffice it to say that you should set yourself apart from the moment you walk through the door by looking fabulous. Now, let's concentrate on attitude.

No Prima Donnas

I can't express enough how damaging a prima donna attitude can be to your work prospects in a myriad of ways. The definition of a diva, at least in my book, is not a whiny, demanding, catty, ungrateful woman who goes around giving us singers a bad name. You can surely see the obvious conflict you'll have if you act this way with those who are directly involved with your performance, like the person running the open mic night, for instance. But the other people with whom you'll come in contact are going to be just as important to treat with respect.

> I want to be a diva . . . like "people-totally-respect-my-music" diva, not like "carry-my-Diet-Coke-around" diva.
>
> *Jessica Simpson*

So many times something like this has happened in my career: I meet a waiter at a restaurant where I am singing who, five years down the road, is the manager of an exclusive club looking for entertainment. Or the valet parking cars at the hotel where I have just finished performing at a wedding reception is engaged, and he and his fiancée are going to need a band. Everyone you come in contact with is a potential boss or client, so treat everyone with the respect they deserve, and your reputation will always precede you in a positive way.

Be Yourself

Also, don't hesitate to be your quirky individual self. I've learned that being a little unusual or not so mainstream sends the message that you are indeed an artist and a force to be reckoned with. For example, I'm often moved to join the audience on the dance floor when another band member is singing or soloing on one of my songs. I've known a singer who likes to perform barefoot, one who has a different hairstyle and/or hair color every other week, and one who wears vintage hats. As long as you aren't being disrespectful or hurting anyone with your idiosyncrasies, you'll add a touch of mystique to your persona, distinguish yourself as an original, and be more memorable to your audience and other musicians.

Etiquette

There are some issues of etiquette you need to be familiar with so that you don't start burning bridges just as you're trying to build a favorable public image. The first issue is regarding when it is and isn't appropriate to sit in with a band. If the event is advertised as an open mic or a jam session, then you are absolutely welcome to give your name and song to the person running the show and sit in for a song or two when called up. However, approaching a band that's performing at a gig and asking if you can sing a song with them is a no-no. Just put it in the context of any other profession, and you'll understand why. You wouldn't go into the kitchen of a restaurant and ask the chef in the middle of his work if he'd mind stepping aside and letting you give it a go.

The extreme of this *faux pas* happened to me when I was

singing in a lounge one evening. While I was right in the middle of a song, a singer came up to the bandleader with her song list and business card in hand to ask if he was looking for a singer, and if so, could she come up and audition right then. (The nerve!) If you are invited to sit in, that's one thing, but otherwise, sit back and be a supportive audience member. The only exception to this rule is if you are at a private function, like your sister's wedding, and she requests that you sing with the band. It's still the band's call, but since your sister is the one paying the band, they'll probably agree.

Diva Sisters

> **GOLDEN RULE**
> *Don't badmouth other singers.*

The second issue of etiquette, as you can see, is a golden rule because it is so important to the longevity of your career. It's only natural that you're going to think of other female singers in your area as your competition. But don't think that by putting other singers down, you are in any way building yourself up. It's much more productive to consider them as your sisters in a sorority. You're all trying to make it in a crazy business, and when you stick together and work as a unified group,

> " I've always defended Shania. She not only opened doors; she knocked several down.
> *Faith Hill*

everyone is stronger. That means passing on a sister's name and number if you're unavailable for a job. Or going to a sister's gig on your night off to show your support.

SHE'S THERE IN TIMES OF NEED

Someday you, too, could be booked to sing for a long-planned, much-anticipated fiftieth anniversary party and suddenly come down with bronchitis. You can call a sister, as I did, to fill in and save your hoarse hide. Or think about the very real possibility that at some point down the road, a gig is going to fall through. It happens all the time (Did I mention that this business is anything but stable?), and when it does, it's comforting to know you have some sisters you can call for leads on other gigs. What goes around, comes around. So before you take the low road, know that eventually, there will be consequences.

> "
> Christina and I are friends, no matter what the media makes up.
> *Britney Spears*
> "

It's All about Relationships

The music business, especially at the local level, is all about relationships. The simple truth is that if people like you, they are much more likely to hire you. So even though at this point you're probably singing for free in amateur venues, don't slack on being a consummate professional. You can bet that when the time comes for auditioning, if you and an equally talented vocalist are up for the same gig, the one who is already known around town to be pleasant and easy to work with, who looks and acts the part, and who already has contacts for future work will get the job.

Self-Promotion

As soon as you begin singing in public, you need to start cultivating a group of loyal fans, so remember these two words: self-promotion. I had an especially hard time with this concept in the beginning of my career because it went against everything I'd been taught as a child. I was raised to be humble, and that to brag about your talents and accomplishments was vulgar. My parents told me to put my energy toward self-improvement, not self-promotion. Well, I don't say this often, but I've discovered that as it applies to show business, my parents were partly wrong. The previous chapters have explained how critical it is to work diligently on honing your craft and striving to be your best. But I'm here to tell you that no matter how incredible your talent, it is still necessary to tell people, be they your audience or prospective employers, just how great you are.

The Talent Rarely Speaks for Itself

I've seen poor performers do well because they are masters at self-promotion, and I've seen far too many great performers do poorly because they lack this skill—it's unfortunate, but the talent rarely speaks for itself. I have one particular vocalist in mind who suffers from a total lack of self-promotion skills. She is, without a doubt, one of the finest singer/songwriters I know, but she remains on the cusp of all the glory and recognition she deserves because she doesn't sell herself. She has recorded and performed with some of the best musicians in her musical genre, and yet she never informs her audience. Instead she halfheartedly holds up her new CD, and says (always in a self-deprecating manner) that they are for sale if anybody wants one.

Share Information

I'm not encouraging the rapper approach here, as in, "I'm the best, and everyone else stinks," but you can graciously grab people's attention by occasionally sharing an anecdote that puts you in a favorable light, a few impressive facts, or simply your gig schedule. In the case of the performer mentioned above, she would sell more CDs, have a more attentive audience, and have a larger following were she to hold her CD up high, and proudly name some of the famous guest artists who are featured with her. In the up-and-coming diva's case, mentioning how excited you are about a future gig and inviting everyone to come, even if it is singing at the elementary school's spaghetti dinner, is a great way to self-promote. It sounds as if you are simply sharing information, but the message is clear that you are proud of your talent and think it is worth coming to see.

Mailing List

TRICK OF THE TRADE
Start a mailing list as soon as possible.

A mailing list is such a simple thing to do, and yet it is so effective for building a fan base. When you have finished singing, just make an announcement that those interested can join your mailing list by leaving a card with you or by writing their name, mailing address, and e-mail address in a small notebook (which you'll have handy, of course) to receive updates of where you'll be performing next.

Whenever you do a public gig, send everyone on your list a notice with the date, time, phone number of the establishment, and good, clear directions. As a reference, you may also want to mention where the person saw you perform last. With everyone on the Internet these days, sending bulk e-mail is the most convenient and cost-effective way to communicate. But for those who don't provide an Internet address, mailing a postcard works just as well. And for a most eye-catching and effective e-mail or postcard, include a great picture of yourself to further jog the recipient's memory of your stunning presence.

Ask Acquaintances

Don't overlook the people in your everyday life as potential supporters who may want to join your mailing list. Your co-workers, schoolmates, dentist, bank teller, neighbors, and the barista at your favorite cafe are already acquaintances, and it couldn't hurt to tell them that you are a singer and to ask if they would like to know where and when you'll be performing. I know that whenever I happen to mention to someone new in my life what I do for a living, there is usually a genuine interest in finding out more details, which is the perfect window of opportunity to get an e-mail address to share information.

The Mailing List Advantage

Believe it or not, people usually feel honored and special when you, the talent, take the time to personally invite them to a show. And if you take the time to acknowledge and thank them if they do accept your invitation, you will have fans for life. If even a small crowd of your admirers comes to a gig, other people in the audience will pick up on their enthusiasm and usually follow suit. Continue adding to your mailing list at every gig, and before you know it, you're going to have a real following, which boils down to job security.

> That's why I work every day. Ev-er-y day. I want to knock people out.
>
> *Aaliyah*

Daily Practice

GOLDEN RULE
Don't stop your daily practice even if you are gigging several nights a week.

In the event that you find yourself singing in a live performance situation several nights a week, don't be tempted to let your practice routine slip. I was guilty of making this mistake twice in my career, and both times I was very sorry. The long-tone exercises and song mastery process as they are detailed in chapters 2 and 5 cannot be neglected, because over time, without practice, you will start to lose your chops (the ability to go from note to note with ease) and endurance.

Most recently, I stopped practicing because I was working five and six nights a week, in addition to doing studio work during the day, and I figured it wasn't necessary anymore. Within two months, I noticed I was having trouble getting through a gig without losing my high- and low-end range. I was also struggling to sing some of the more challenging songs in my repertoire, and I felt a general loss of control. When I realized what was happening, I went back to practicing five mornings a week between twenty and thirty minutes, and I was soon back where I wanted to be. A day or two of rest is healthy when you are performing a lot, but don't drop your practice routine completely.

Growing Pains

At this juncture, I must mention that you need to be ready for the possibility of some growing pains. There is nothing that can totally prepare you for singing in front of an audience. Songs that you feel you've mastered at home, when sung for the first time in public, may sound weak at best. There are so many variables in a live performance that are not present at home. Take typical performance jitters and then add people talking, or chairs scraping, or dishes clanging, or pool balls smacking together while the jukebox plays on (Ouch, that still smarts), and then throw in obnoxious revelers, or unruly children, or hecklers yelling song requests, or worse.

The Myth

Once you begin performing in public, you will soon discover a myth that has been perpetuated in practically every movie lounge scene ever made. In the real world, audience members do not always sit with big smiles on their faces, bobbing their heads in time to the music, and listening attentively to the singer they are hearing for the first time. Nor do they always erupt in thunderous applause and enthusiastic whistles as the last note fades away. And the singer doesn't then come off the stage after just one song to be embraced and fawned over by the adoring crowd. It takes lots of experience and seasoning along with shameless self-promotion before a singer can hope to get that kind of Hollywood response.

The Less-than-Glamorous Side

And while I'm being honest about the less-than-glamorous side of this profession, get used to the fact that not everyone is going to like you, and some people will be sure to let you know it. I've had people cover their ears, hold their noses, and walk off the dance floor in obvious disgust. People have told me to do something with my hair, to never wear a particular outfit again, and have actually asked whether I'd gained weight since they last saw me, among other atrocities. For some reason, there are always those in an audience who think that your being onstage gives them license to do and say anything to you. If you can, ignore and carry on, but if someone becomes too obnoxious or offensive, you can always walk off the stage. This is a luxury you have early on since you're probably singing for free, so use it. When you are the paid performer, as I'll talk about in chapter 9, it will be necessary to handle things differently.

Adjustment Period

With all of these changes, is it any wonder, then, that you'll need an adjustment period? Don't get discouraged! You are in the company of many great divas who had to "fail" over and over before they conquered live performance. It's all a part of paying your dues, and although it may get better, it never ends. I once paid good money for a second-row seat in a large concert hall to see one

> What's meant to be will always find a way.
> *Trisha Yearwood*

of my favorite world-class divas in concert. I was so excited to see her up close and personal, but the man sitting in front of me in the first row obviously wasn't. He literally fell asleep at her feet while she sang her heart out. At one point she looked down at him, gave a little chuckle, and proceeded to give a brilliant performance. Forge ahead. Practice singing in public. Try out your material. It's only a matter of time before singing in front of an audience, receptive or otherwise, will feel natural to you.

Don't Fret

If finding an opportunity to experience live performance doesn't happen right away, don't fret. I am a firm believer that when the diva is ready, the gig will appear. Continue working on yourself, becoming so fabulous and irresistible that, before long, people will be calling you to perform at their functions. Stay highly visible by continuing to frequent live music venues and your local music stores, and be persistently, unabashedly vocal about telling anyone and everyone your desire to sing.

Comfort Food

I want to give you one last bit of comfort (food) before I summarize because it is likely that the steps in this chapter will be the most challenging in your diva journey thus far. This is the internship stage of your new job, and even though you have voluntarily sought the position and are excited about the work, all change is stressful. Eating delicious and healthy meals is one of the best coping mechanisms I know of to deal with stress, so even though a pint of New York Super Fudge Chunk ice cream may seem more in keeping with comfort food, this salad is truly going to nurture you.

TASTY TIDBIT: YOU GO GIRL SALAD *(SINGLE SERVING)*
* ❋ *burger-size portion of lean ground beef*
* ❋ *2 teaspoons olive oil*
* ❋ *½ small onion, chopped*
* ❋ *1 large clove garlic, minced*
* ❋ *1 tablespoon Worcestershire sauce*
* ❋ *2 cups romaine lettuce*
* ❋ *5 grape or cherry tomatoes*
* ❋ *shredded cheddar cheese*
* ❋ *salt and pepper to taste*

*In a skillet over medium high heat, brown beef, onions, and garlic
with the olive oil and worcestershire sauce until meat is cooked
through. Season with salt and pepper to taste, and pour mixture
over lettuce and tomato, and sprinkle with cheese. Toss with a little
Ranch or Blue Cheese dressing.*

To Sum It Up

In this chapter, I've given you several general leads for finding and
creating opportunities to sing in your area, in addition to some coping mechanisms to deal with these new experiences. With life in the
public eye comes scrutiny, so I've also armed you with rules of etiquette and tips for creating a favorable image right out of the box.
Don't beat yourself up if your first performance experiences don't
measure up to Hollywood's version. Just try to remember why you
began this journey in the first place—to pursue your passion to
sing—and isn't that exactly what you are finally doing? So check
your ego at the door, forget every idea you've ever had about appropriate audience response, and sing. It truly is its own reward.

A DIVA NEXT DOOR SAYS
*Always be prepared before you sit in at a jam session.
This doesn't require you to have a degree in music,
but every singer should arm herself with some basic
music knowledge and theory before she attempts to join
other musicians in an impromptu situation. Know your song keys,
the song form and style, and be able to count off the tempo and end
the song. If you really want to be prepared, you can even bring
charts. By doing a little homework, you'll save yourself from a
potentially embarrassing situation, and you'll be comfortable
enough to actually enjoy the experience. —Nicole*

CHAPTER 7

A Woman's Worth

INVESTMENTS IN YOUR FUTURE SUCCESS

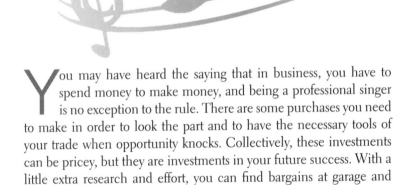

You may have heard the saying that in business, you have to spend money to make money, and being a professional singer is no exception to the rule. There are some purchases you need to make in order to look the part and to have the necessary tools of your trade when opportunity knocks. Collectively, these investments can be pricey, but they are investments in your future success. With a little extra research and effort, you can find bargains at garage and school sales, on the Internet, in the newspaper's classified ads, at discount stores, and simply by asking other singers and musicians.

Music Purchases

Your first purchase should be a quality vocal microphone. If you have spent any time in the music store or online looking at microphones, you know they vary considerably in price. While you don't want to scrimp on this purchase, keep in mind that the most expensive mic isn't necessarily the best one for your voice. Some mics are better suited to an alto range while others have more "bottom" to balance a soprano voice. Make inquiries of other female vocalists who sing in your range, and ask the salespeople at the music store for suggestions. A standard, relatively inexpensive microphone that many professional lead and backup singers use for performance is the Shure SM58—it is a solid choice for your first microphone. I started with and am still using the Electro Voice N/D 767, which is another dependable vocal mic and one which I feel compliments my alto voice. Finally, take the time to test different models and trust your ear to guide you to the one that gives your unique voice a full, balanced sound.

Stands and a Gig Bag

Your next purchases should be a microphone stand, a music stand, and a gig bag, which is a large, sturdy, multipurpose duffel you'll need in order to carry smaller items like your binder, microphone, percussion instruments, and so forth, to a gig. These items are relatively inexpensive but highly functional.

Percussion Instruments

While you're at the music store, look into buying a few more percussion instruments as well. A tambourine, claves, cabasa, or even a cowbell are all options that can add to your value as a performer. Percussion instruments can make a performance more visually exciting for the audience, and if done well, can greatly add to the sound of the band. Practice at home, and once you get with a band, ask the drummer in rehearsal to help you with improving your technique.

TRICK OF THE TRADE
While playing your percussion instruments onstage, keep them well away from the microphone until your ability improves.

By keeping your percussion instruments away from the mic, you'll still get to practice your skills and you'll get the visual benefits to your stage presence. But if you mess up, you won't be throwing the time off for the other musicians, or worse, sullying the music for the audience.

Wardrobe

Next comes a wardrobe fit for the stage, and when shopping for yours, keep this in mind.

GOLDEN RULE
Never, ever dress like an audience member.

As surprising as it may seem, both the audience and business owners are adamant about the performer looking the part by being dressed in something showy, even costume-like, so don't disappoint them. One time, a patron actually complained to the manager of the club where I was singing because I was wearing a dressy pantsuit instead of a dress. I didn't necessarily agree with the gripe, but it did make me realize how much the audience pays attention to what I wear.

> I modeled my looks on the town tramp.
> *Dolly Parton*

Job Title: Vocalist

As an adult, I didn't dress the way I really wanted to until I started singing. Somehow the fact that my job title changed to "vocalist" gave me the license I needed to buy the more theatrical clothes that I'd always favored but hadn't felt confident enough to wear. I'll never forget sauntering into a department store shortly after getting my first official paycheck and buying a long black cape. One look and my head swam with glorious visions of throwing that cape ever so dramatically over my shoulders as I made a grand exit from a successful gig. That simple accessory appealed to my sense of beauty and fantasy and was the first step toward claiming my individual diva style.

> Being in a band, you can wear whatever you want—it's like an excuse for Halloween every day.
> *Gwen Stefani*

Consult the Child Within

Be playful rather than practical in your purchases. It's helpful to recall your state of mind as a little girl when you knew exactly what you loved and weren't afraid to wear it. As a child, I remember begging my mother for red sparkly shoes like Dorothy's in *The Wizard of Oz*. She finally agreed to buy me red sandals as a compromise. I put those shoes by my bed every night that summer so that I could put them on the moment I awoke each morning. The point is, the little girl in all of us knows exactly what she loves, so listen to her!

One online shop that's all about playfulness is Fred Flare (visit *www.FredFlare.com* or call 718-599-9221). This funky, offbeat cyberboutique has very reasonably priced showtime accessories and tons of fun knickknacks. And the best part is, much of its merchandise is pop music oriented, like the Cher necklace and the Stevie Nicks earrings, both of which would adorn any diva well.

Diva Style

A diva comes in all shapes and sizes, with clothing preferences ranging from blue jeans to boas. But the one constant is her intuitive sense of personal style and the confidence to wear what looks and feels great on her, convention be damned! Diva style isn't a formula, it's a freedom to capture your uniqueness in dress. Chrissie Hynde is all about rocker clothes in dark colors. Natalie Cole always achieves a sexy elegance in her body-hugging gowns. What will your diva style be?

You can answer that question by buying one article of clothing or accessory at a time that calls to you—a diva style starter, if you will. It needs to draw you in at an emotional level, such as the color being your favorite shade of blue, or the cut accentuating an especially gifted body part you are most proud of. No need to spend a lot of money here (thrift and consignment stores are treasure-troves), but you do need to make an effort to buy something a little over-the-top so that you can start defining your look.

Diva Style Starters

* ❋ A little black dress
* ❋ Black pants that fit to thrill
* ❋ A cape, scarf, boa, or anything that can be dramatically draped over your shoulders
* ❋ A conversation piece of costume jewelry
* ❋ High heels in a bright or metallic color
* ❋ Big, dark sunglasses that suggest a star incognito
* ❋ Any piece of clothing with sequins, sparkle, or shine

Free Clothes

You'll need to file away this next bit of exciting information for future reference, but under no circumstances should you forget it because I'm talking about free clothes. Once you begin performing at the most happening, hottest, and swankiest places around town (which I have no doubt you will), you should ask some area retailers if they would like to loan you an outfit in exchange for some great advertisement. Tell them that whenever you wear that store's apparel on a gig, you will have a small sign displayed on the stage that says who your clothes have been provided by. Some stores will

> I've always loved long flowing clothes. I used to rummage around in my grandmother's trunks trying to find them.
> *Stevie Nicks*

let you borrow a designer outfit for an evening if you hand out their cards. Local boutiques are usually more receptive to this idea than the bigger chains, but it never hurts to ask.

Polishers

I'm going to clue you in now on a few little extra touches, or polishers as I call them, that make a big difference in your overall appearance. If you've ever watched *American Idol* on TV, you've probably witnessed the metamorphosis that the contestants go through once the show's stylists get a hold of them. The most obvious areas of improvement are hair and makeup, but I'm convinced it's also the more subtle details that define a diva look.

Undergarments

First on the list is to purchase proper undergarments for your new wardrobe. I don't care if you break the bank to buy the most perfectly flattering little black dress known to man, if your bust isn't well supported in the front and you've got panty lines showing in the back, then your dress is going to look cheap, both coming and going. Control-top pantyhose to the rescue! They eliminate those unsightly ripples caused by standard issue underwear. Or if you'd rather bare your legs, you can go with a thong or one of the body shapers (basically a control top without the stockings) underneath.

BOOB JOB IN A BOX

Now I'll divulge to you one of the greatest contributions to lingerie of all time: Nu Bra™ fashion forms. I'll never forget the day I got the call from my diva girlfriend. It began with the question, "Are you sitting down?" We had both been complaining for years about not being able to find the perfect, all-purpose, formalwear bra. Practically out of breath with excitement, she proceeded to tell me about these miraculous, self-adhesive, nearly invisible bra cups, and how they worked beautifully (meaning they made her look naturally perkier and fuller) with all her backless and strapless tops and dresses. The news of her discovery spread like wildfire throughout the diva community, and soon we all looked better in our stage clothes. Just so you know what you're looking for, they look like two chicken cutlets, and they're available to you in most fine department stores and lingerie shops. I've noticed recently that some of the chain drugstores are carrying other, less expensive brands.

Bronzers

For those of you who are blessed with even-toned gorgeous skin, this next polisher isn't for you. For the rest of us, a sunless tanning product found in any drugstore works wonders. Use it to cover bathing suit lines on your shoulders and back or wherever you need to even out skin tone. For an overall healthy glow, you can apply it from head to toe, but follow the directions carefully. If you don't exfoliate first or are too heavy-handed or haphazard in the application, your skin can end up looking orange and blotchy. The color lasts for at least a few days, so don't start experimenting with a self-tanner the day before a gig.

Hair

Your hairstyle has to match the rest of you, which means the head-band and the scrunchie are out of the question. You need a glamo-rous, flattering "do," so seek the guidance and service of a professional hairdresser. Get to your appointment early so you can thumb through the hairstyle magazines. A picture is critical when you're trying to describe to your hairdresser the look you're after. Your idea of a little trim could be two inches different from hers, and we all know how miserable that little misunderstanding can be. Also, ask what products are being used and watch closely how to style your hair so that you can get that "just-walked-out-of-a-salon" look at home. With a little practice, you'll be styling your hair like a pro.

COLOR

It's amazing what a few highlights, lowlights, or a subtle hair color change can do to enhance your eye color, make your skin glow, and even take years off your overall appearance. Again, I would highly recommend consulting a professional. I once made the mistake of deciding I wanted to be a redhead the day of a gig. My hair ended up a Ronald McDonald red rather than the glorious auburn shade shown on the box, and I had no choice but to show up at the very elegant engagement party sporting clown hair. It goes without saying that it wasn't one of my best moments, although the band did find it very entertaining.

Makeup

In keeping with the goal of oozing star quality from every pore, your makeup should follow suit and be a little flashier and heavier than your everyday look.

GOLDEN RULE
Your stage makeup should include one of the three S': shimmer, sparkle, or shine. Cosmetics that reflect light produce a luminous glow in the spotlight.

I learned how to create a dramatic stage face by having my makeup done at a department store's cosmetics counter. Usually, a makeover is free with no obligation to buy the products (it actually looks good for them to have people sitting at the counter), but you'll probably want to purchase a few items so you can recreate the look yourself. To make sure you have plenty of time to ask questions and won't be rushed through, plan to visit the counter during department store downtimes, which are generally weekdays in the morning right after opening and mid-afternoon.

Another option is to pick up one of the many how-to books on makeup application so you'll have a handy reference to consult for creating several different looks. My favorite book is *Making Faces* by the late, great, makeup-artist-to-the-stars, Kevyn Aucoin. It has several examples of the striking looks that I'm usually going for. Or go to the most fun makeup superstore on the planet, Sephora. If you've never been there, it's like a big cosmetics candy store where they allow you to try everything before you buy. Even if you aren't near a store, sign up online at *www.sephora.com* or call 1-800-SEPHORA to receive the free seasonal catalogs by mail. Every issue has expert step-by-step instructions along with product information for several different of-the-moment looks.

Mani and Pedi

If you think I'm talking about two extras from the *Sopranos*, then we definitely need to talk. I'm referring to pretty fingers and toes here. Again, it's the little touches, like clean, well-groomed fingernails and toenails, that make for a totally glam look. At the minimum, keep your nails evenly filed with a coat of clear polish (my personal preference because it's fast and easy). And for those ultra-formal gigs, you may want to have your nails done.

PRACTICAL GEM
Go to a nail school for a deeply discounted manicure and pedicure.

Once you've gotten your hands and feet cleaned up and in shape at a nail school, you can extend the life of your professional mani and pedi by doing some at-home maintenance. Hang nails and dry heels can be avoided by liberally applying Vaseline to your hands and feet and then covering them with cotton socks and gloves at bedtime. And when the color starts looking dull or you get a chip, file the nail in one direction following the existing shape, gently push back cuticles with an orange stick, and then apply a fresh coat of cheap nail polish in a similar color.

Eyebrows

Let's not leave the salon so fast. If you've never had your brows shaped by a professional, you haven't even begun to realize the full beauty of your face. Well-shaped eyebrows act as a complementary frame for all your facial features, but the eyes benefit the most. They can open up the eye area, making small eyes appear larger and adding width to close-set eyes. Even if you have perfectly symmetrical peepers, getting your eyebrows shaped allows for easier, better makeup application. No diva makeover is complete without this.

> "Making miracles is hard work. Most people give up before they happen.
> *Sheryl Crow*"

High Fashion

I know it's starting to sound like dressing and primping for a gig will be the equivalent of taking on a small construction project, but stay with me. There's just one more polisher needed to give you that cutting edge, "thumb-on-the-pulse-of-fashion" look: a hip and trendy accessory. Look through fashion magazines for the latest fads hitting the streets and runways. Then, go to your local discount department or thrift store to find an inexpensive look-alike.

I once picked up a Tiffany-inspired bracelet from a sale table for eight bucks. I'd seen them worn in the magazines by different celebrities and was thrilled with my find. At the time, I was singing in an exclusive club where sometimes even royalty came in. That night, Lord and Lady S were enjoying a dance when the Lady spied my new bracelet. She gushed on and on with so many compliments that I finally told her how much it cost and gave it to her. You'd have thought I'd given her the real thing by her response, and she showed her appreciation with a hefty tip before leaving. You don't want to go overboard and wear every fad that will fit on your person, but just one well-coordinated, trendy accessory will keep that little black dress looking fresh and current.

A Diva Résumé

Now that you have the tools of your trade and you look the part, you need to invest in a résumé that will represent your talent, dedication, and professionalism in the most flattering manner possible. The ideal singer's résumé includes a brief cover letter/bio, an eight-by-ten-inch, black-and-white headshot (a picture from the neck up), your song list, a business card, and a three-to-five-song demo. Many times, before a live audition, agents, bands, or businesses will ask for this type of package so they can narrow down their candidates. When presented this way, your résumé immediately communicates that you are a serious player.

Résumé Contents

* Cover letter/bio
* Black-and-white, eight-by-ten inch headshot
* Three- to five-song demo
* Song list
* Business card

Cover Letter/Bio

The cover letter/bio should be brief and to the point (see appendix B). Put your name and phone number centered at the top of the page, followed by your performance experience. Even if it's limited, present your history in the most glowing terms (without lying, of course), and then highlight any positives, such as your willingness to travel, or your flexible schedule for rehearsals and gigs, or even your minivan that could be used for hauling equipment. Don't be afraid to show your personality or humor in your writing. Chances are, your package won't be the only one being considered, so anything that makes yours memorable is a plus. Once you gain more work experience, a separate cover letter and bio will be more appropriate, but for starters, combining the two works well.

Professional Photo

Have a photo taken by a professional not only because it will be the first visual impression your prospective employers will have of you, but also because there's a possibility that the picture could be used for publicity purposes once you've gotten the gig.

I asked a friend who was a shutterbug to take my first photo— big mistake. Sure, it was good enough to send out to bands in answer to their "vocalist needed" ads in the paper. It served its purpose of assuring them that I was the age I claimed to be and not hideously unattractive. But when the band that hired me enlarged the snapshot and attached it to the poster at the front of the club, I was mortified. Customers came up to me all night, saying that I looked nothing like my picture. Believe me, I took it as a huge compliment. We made plans that night to go and have a professional band photo taken.

The Pro Advantage

Only you know what works with your budget, and I understand that it's hard at this stage to keep forking out money with nothing coming in. But if you can swing it, go to a professional photographer. Look through some different portfolios, shopping around for someone who has worked with bands and entertainers before. A good photographer will ask you questions about your personality and style of music and then use the information to suggest backgrounds and poses. The better studios also have makeup artists on staff that you can book for your session, making for an even better publicity shot. An expert will apply the most flattering makeup for black-and-white photography so that you won't look too harsh or washed out in the photo.

Song Demo

The three- to five-song demo is your audio calling card. It should be a clearly recorded cassette or CD that showcases your range, versatility, and ability to sell a song. Before going to an expensive commercial recording studio, however, investigate some other options. These days, many musicians have sophisticated home studios and some karaoke stores have recording facilities, both with more reasonable hourly rates than a professional recording studio. To further cut costs, bring your own karaoke music tracks to the songs you want to record so you won't have to pay for an accompanist.

I go into more detail about recording in chapter 10, but the most important thing is to make sure you go into the studio knowing your material. Tell the engineer that this is your first time so she can give you some guidance. And try to stay relaxed. If your voice is shaky from nerves, you won't be able to get a recording that accurately shows your beautiful talent, and that is, after all, the goal.

PRACTICAL GEM
Instead of recording the entire song, just record the first verse and the chorus.

By recording only part of each song, you will not only cut down on your expenses, but future auditioners will be grateful that you showed your talent in a succinct manner.

Song List

Your song list will be easiest to read if you break it down into style categories. Under such headings as disco, jazz, rock, country, Broadway, Latin, etc., put your songs in alphabetical order. Pick your brain and make sure you include not only the songs you've mastered, but also the songs you are somewhat familiar with. There will be time after you get the gig to brush up on any sketchy material on the list that the band wants to include in its repertoire, so name them all. More songs just look more impressive.

Name Change?

Here's a little something to ponder as you're on the verge of going fully public and before you have everything printed. Is a name change in order? Does your name accurately reflect the image that you're trying to project? At the local level, it may be most advantageous for you to keep your name exactly as it is so you can use your name recognition as a draw. On the other hand, if your name is too ordinary, hard to pronounce, or awkward in any way, now might be a good time to come up with your new stage name. I've known performers to drop their last names, add their middle names, or use their initials to come up with an acronym. Others just throw caution to the wind and come up with something new altogether. Give this some serious thought, because a catchy, memorable name is very important in show business.

Assembly

The cover letter/bio, song list, and business cards can be printed either on your home computer, if you have the capabilities, or at a print shop. As long as the text is clearly legible, you can have some fun in choosing the typeface and creating a design to complement the image you want to project. If you really want to impress, package everything in a two-pocket colored folder with a three-hole binder in the center. First, using your business card as a template in the center of the left pocket, lightly pencil in a mark just below the top left and bottom right corners. Remove the business card and then use an exacto knife to make two small cuts in the pocket where you marked with the pencil. Now slip in the two corresponding corners of your business card. Three-hole-punch your cover letter/bio and song list respectively, and secure with the three prongs inside the binder so the cover letter is seen first. And finally, put your photo in the left pocket and your CD or cassette in the right pocket.

Get the Word Out

There are any number of ways that you can go about getting work if you just think outside the box a little bit. The next chapter deals with the more traditional way in which a band forms and gets gigs—by an audition process and through agents. But now that you have your diva résumé ready, you're familiar with the local music scene, and you've made so many contacts, you can also try going straight to the source. Personally deliver your packages to clubs and restaurants, lodges, and bars—anywhere that has entertainment or any place you think should have entertainment. Create a gig by convincing the proprietor to give you a night to prove that you can draw more customers. If you get a bite, and someone wants to hire you, it's a lot easier to get a band together when you have a promising gig already lined up. Then, contact every person on your mailing list, and ask them to come out to support you.

Hand out packages to co-workers, friends, family members, and neighbors, and ask them to pass the information on to anyone they know who might be interested. Put up notices on strategic bulletin boards, call talent agents to see if they know of any band openings, put an ad in an entertainment rag announcing that an accomplished vocalist is looking to form a band. Generally, get the word out to anyone who'll listen that you are a vocalist-for-hire and officially in business!

To Sum It Up

You're really getting down to business now as you become financially committed to your goal. With each purchase you make that is listed in this chapter, picture your phone ringing off the hook with calls coming in from eager employers because they've received your résumé package and are totally impressed. Picture yourself onstage, sounding and looking incredible because you've invested in professional gear and seen to every detail of your appearance. And don't forget to keep all of your receipts for diva-related purchases. I have a feeling that when tax time rolls around, your income from singing will be such that you'll be needing to take all the deductions you can.

A DIVA NEXT DOOR SAYS

Always show respect to your band. We chick singers get a bad rap from time to time because of a few bad eggs. Don't just waltz in five minutes before showtime and plug in your microphone. Come early to help with the setup and stay late for the breakdown, even if it's just to roll cords and carry stands. The band is working hard behind you, but because they aren't the featured vocalist, many times the audience doesn't give them the credit they deserve. Make sure they do by introducing each member by name at some point in the gig. Don't start talking to someone in the audience when an instrumentalist plays a solo. Pay attention and listen. If you are given a cash tip, even if it is handed to you personally while you are on a break, split it equally among the band members. All these things make for good relations and a happy band that will play to make you sound your best. —Lisa

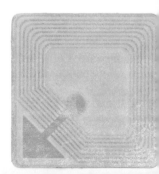

The Chorus

Hallelujah, the Diva Is Revealed!

The Chorus

To live my life like a butterfly,
Knowing that my days are precious few,
Listening to the whispers of my beating heart's desire,
And gracefully make my dreams come true.

The chorus is always the glorious high point and the ultimate destination of a song, and if you've succeeded in completing phases 1 and 2, you are definitely at your personal peak. Phase 3 is all about how to ride the wave and stay on top, by making the most and getting the most out of every opportunity. I give you the scoop on how to shine at your auditions, how to negotiate a deal with an agent, and how to have highly successful gigs. I also give you numerous ways to step your game up to the next level.

And if you're interested in dropping the "next door" from your title, I share some sound advice and concrete leads to get you started on your way to superstardom. In phase 3, I drive home the point that no matter which direction you choose to take your career, the diva philosophy of listening to your heart, taking risks, and continuing to seek knowledge and growth should always prevail.

CHAPTER 8

A Star Is Born

SHINING AT YOUR AUDITION

N ow that you have a solid song repertoire, a dazzling diva wardrobe, and the attitude to match, it's time to step onto the stage and show 'em what you're made of. It's audition time! This is both exciting and a bit nerve-wracking. But if you approach every audition as another opportunity to learn and gain experience, you'll never be disappointed. In fact, the more auditions (even if they aren't for exactly the type of gig you're after), the better. Anything, no matter how small, can turn into something bigger or lead to more desirable opportunities.

> You get nervous with no one supporting you. People don't always have the vision, and the secret for the person with the vision is to stand up. It takes a lot of courage.
>
> *Natalie Cole*

The Process

Let's walk through this process step by step. You have sent your résumé (folder with picture, demo, etc.) and naturally gotten the call to come in for a live audition. While you have the person on the phone, ask some questions:

❋ Will you be auditioning in front of a live audience or at the band's rehearsal space?
❋ Will the band have an operating sound system for you to plug your microphone into?
❋ Is the band familiar with songs on your song list?
❋ Can someone accompany you?
❋ Or if not, do they want you to sing a capella or with your own karaoke CDs?

Getting all the particulars will help you to be as prepared as possible. And to help you organize your thoughts to be able to ask the right questions, I've listed below the three main audition call questions. The answers to these will lead you to more specific questions, and ultimately a solid plan for the audition.

Audition Call Questions

❋ Where and what time?
❋ How many and what style of songs will I be expected to sing?
❋ What do I need to bring?

A Band of One

If you didn't notice when you were on your field trips to live music venues, a "band" these days may only consist of one person playing an accompanying instrument and a machine that plays the supplementary music. The machine providing the music can be any number of things from a sequencer, to a minidisc player, to a laptop computer, or even a CD player for karaoke music tracks. The current reality is that technology has made obsolete the necessity to hire a full band of live musicians in order to play pop music. And because a one-man (electronically enhanced) band charges less than a five-piece live band, individuals and businesses will often go for the less expensive alternative. So don't be surprised if, when you go to your audition, the "band" turns out to be one person and a machine.

Be Safe

Use your common sense, or that sixth sense, to tell you if anything feels uncomfortable or less than kosher with the audition. I'm glad to say that I have no cautionary tales to share, but perhaps it's because I've always followed two rules. First, try to get a reference from one of your contacts if the audition is with someone you are unfamiliar with. And second, unless your audition is in a safe, public place, always bring along a friend.

Choosing Audition Songs

Now, choose three of your strongest songs to showcase, preferably a ballad, a mid-tempo song, and an up-tempo tune. Zero-in on the songs that you're most comfortable singing and that show your special qualities, like a dynamic range or a beautiful tone.

GOLDEN RULE
Don't pick audition songs that have been over-done—like "Feelings" or the theme from Titanic *—or songs that don't fit stylistically with the band you're auditioning for. Both will annoy your auditioner, so don't chance it.*

Once you've decided on the songs, rehearse them like crazy! If you have the time and opportunity, perform your songs in front of an audience. You want to be able to sing these songs forward, backward, and in your sleep, so that come audition time, you'll be so prepared that nothing short of a natural disaster will keep you from singing your best.

Take a Break

Once you've practiced adequately, laid out the perfect outfit, and packed your gig bag with everything you'll need for the audition, it's time to take a break. Overpreparation can be as detrimental to your performance as slacking off, because you can strain your voice and/or work yourself into an exhausted mess—definitely not the first impression you want to make. To keep some balance, it's best to get away from rehearsing for awhile and engage in a calming, meditative activity like walking, knitting, yoga, or cooking. I can always get into a zen-like zone when I'm chopping and assembling ingredients for something delicious like these Showtime Egg Rolls, and the end result is a peaceful mind and a happy belly.

TASTY TIDBIT: SHOWTIME EGG ROLLS
* ❊ 1 package all-purpose pasta wraps
* ❊ 1 tablespoon olive oil
* ❊ 1 bag (16 oz.) precut broccoli or cabbage slaw
* ❊ ½ lb. chicken, beef, pork, or shrimp, cut in bite-size pieces
* ❊ 1 medium onion, chopped
* ❊ 1 clove garlic, minced
* ❊ 1 tablespoon soy sauce
* ❊ ½ teaspoon pepper

Preheat oven to 350°. In a large pot on medium high heat, stir fry meat, onions, garlic, and slaw in olive oil until cooked through. (If using shrimp, stir fry veggies 5 minutes before adding the meat.) Just before removing from burner, mix in soy sauce and pepper. Place one cup of mixture in the center of each pasta wrap and roll up from corner to corner. Secure ends by tucking them inside.

Lightly grease cookie sheet with cooking spray, and place rolls seam side down. Bake until golden brown, approximately 30 to 35 minutes. Serve with ginger dressing, hot mustard, soy sauce, or duck sauce. Makes 8 to 10 rolls.

The Day Has Arrived

The day has arrived, and you're ready to show your stuff. I'll now describe a cleansing ritual I do before every gig. It is so effective for washing away any negativity and stress of the day, getting calm, centered, and warmed up, and it also works as a transition from my daytime persona (wife, mother, homemaker, carpool driver, etc.) to diva. I think you'll come to agree that it is an absolute necessity before any performance.

Cleansing Ritual

❊ Draw a hot, steamy bath, adding some fragrant beads or bubbles, light a candle, and dim the lights.

❊ While you're bathing, do some positive visualization by picturing yourself in minute detail at the audition or gig singing in top form and impressing your audience.

❊ Before you leave the steamy confines of the tub, do a five-minute vocal warm-up.

First Impressions

You know how important first impressions are, so even if the audition is taking place in someone's garage, dress the part. I'm not saying you need to don the beaded gown, but definitely be neat and choose an outfit with some flash. It goes without saying that you should be prompt and ready to go, with a positive, professional attitude. As prepared as you try to be, however, expect the unexpected.

I remember going to an audition at a club one evening where the band was auditioning several singers. When the singer before me realized she wasn't the only one there that night, she barked at the bandleader that she didn't realize the audition was going to be *Star Search*. I'll admit it was a little unnerving having the other candidates in the audience while I auditioned, but I sucked it up and kept that all-important positive, professional attitude. Guess who got the gig?

Run with "Mistakes"

Bottom line: It ain't brain surgery. If you make a "mistake" during your audition, no one will die. If you have fun with it, a so-called mistake can be even more entertaining than putting on a perfect performance. When I first started performing, I thought the most important objective was to hit every note and remember the lyrics— in essence, to sing perfectly. Boring. By watching and listening to the divas I admired, I soon learned how flaws added so much to the entertainment value and allowed their humanity to shine through. My favorite example is when Ella Fitzgerald in her *Live in Berlin* concert forgot the words to "Mack the Knife" and made up her own to the delight of the audience. She ran with her "mistake" and ended up bringing down the house. Of course, band members are looking for a fine vocalist who fits their style of music, but equally as important, they are looking for someone they can enjoy working with week after week.

Tell Your Story

Remember that singing is an art that in its highest form evokes some emotion within you and your audience. This is true whether you are singing in Carnegie Hall or auditioning in someone's basement. Dig deep and find the meaning of the song you are singing, and then give it your own personal soul injection. Tony award®–winner Linda Lavin, whose character on the sitcom *Alice* was the original "diva next door" (and who continues to give moving performances in theater, in cabaret, and on TV), put it most eloquently: "Learn to tell the story of the song, to express your own stories from your heart, and your voice will follow and be true."

> I didn't write these songs, but I can relate to every one of them. It's soul music—I have to feel it in order to sing it with a little bit of soul.
>
> *Joss Stone*

Top Ten Audition Mistakes

* Arriving late
* Not coming prepared with enough material
* Not bringing the necessary gear (e.g., microphone, karaoke CDs, etc.)
* Being unprofessional
* Being uncooperative
* Singing unflattering or overdone songs
* Wearing sloppy or inappropriate attire
* Requesting to "start over" in the middle of a song
* Demanding to know immediately if you got the job
* Failing to graciously thank the auditioner

Be Discerning

At this point in your diva journey, you would probably go to the ends of the earth for an opportunity to sing with a band. But don't let your eagerness cloud your judgment. When you go to an audition, you should also be interviewing the band to see if your personalities and goals are compatible. Musicians, as in every other profession, can be egomaniacs, control freaks, substance abusers, and/or womanizers. Weigh the positives and the negatives carefully so you don't get yourself in a situation that keeps you from growing and learning or one that is potentially harmful.

Steady Gig

Aside from determining that you'll be in a relatively healthy, functional band, one of the most important objectives you'll want to have in common with the other members is the intention of getting one consistent venue in which to perform. No matter how lowly the dive or crazy the hour, the public needs to know where to find you on a weekly basis or there is no way you are going to be able to build a following. Sure, private parties pay more, but in the long run, a steady Tuesday night at the local watering hole will allow you to develop a fan base, which is crucial for any band to stay in business.

Beware of Band Romance

> I think we just feel like we want to play places and enjoy music for what it is and not be overambitious and conquer the world.
> *Amy Ray of the Indigo Girls*

So let's assume that you and your potential bandmates are on the same page as far as work ethic and goals, everyone is getting along famously, and it looks like it's going to be a musical match made in heaven. Well, get ready for the very real potential that Cupid's arrows are going to fly. Making music together is heady stuff, and it can be deceptive by making two people believe there is something more between them than just good musical chemistry. Now, understand that this advice is coming from a woman who married her favorite accompanist, but think very carefully before getting involved with a band member. A fling for one person may feel like the love of a lifetime to another, and there the troubles begin. Look at the long-term effects of your actions, especially if you're in a band that is working well together, building a following, and playing steady gigs. And then ask yourself if you would be willing to give all of that up if the relationship went sour. I know there is little rationale involved when it comes to love or lust, but you can't say I didn't warn you.

Business Sense

Now for some much-needed business sense. Up to this point, we have been focusing on developing your talent so that you can get the work. But great talent alone will not ensure your success. In order to turn that talent into financial gain, you need to know the ropes.

> **PRACTICAL GEM**
> *Get an idea of the pay scale for vocalists in your area by asking around.*

Negotiating Your Fee

When negotiating your fee (always before the gig), the number of hours, travel distance, and type of occasion should be considered. For instance, a Saturday night, five-hour wedding gig that requires you to be the master of ceremonies, learn two new songs, and make a two-hour commute should pay more than a steady, Wednesday night, three-hour gig at the neighborhood bar and grill.

> " I'm tough, ambitious, and I know exactly what I want.
> *Madonna* "

Also, inquire about the band or the gig's break and overtime policies. I usually try for fifteen-minute breaks on the hour or the equivalent in an evening. Occasionally, however, certain parties will request that you work a "continuous," as it's called in the business. This means that live music is provided continuously throughout the gig, with the band taking five-minute breaks one member at a time while the others continue performing. If overtime (O.T.) is required, the pay should be time-and-a-half for each additional set. Both "continuous" and "O.T." scenarios are extra work, so make sure you'll be duly compensated.

Booking Yourself

Good contracts make for good business relationships, and if you're booking yourself, insist that you get everything in writing in the form of a performance agreement. (See appendix C for a basic contract, which you are welcome to use as a template to create your own legal document for the services you plan to provide. However, it is not intended to be a substitute for personalized advice from a knowledgeable lawyer in your state.) I've learned the hard way that a phone conversation doesn't always cut it. A mere verbal agreement can, at the very least, result in a miscommunication on the time of the affair or the number of breaks for instance, and at the most, result in not getting paid at all.

I once made arrangements with a caterer over the phone to perform at a four-hour backyard wedding reception. The day arrived with a strong forecast for thunderstorms, but the bride insisted that the band set up outside under a small tent as planned nonetheless. After two hours of rain blowing in on us, puddles began dangerously forming around the electrical cords—and our feet. That, coupled with some close lightning strikes, forced us to pull the plug and seek shelter for safety reasons. We waited inside for the storm to pass, but it continued through the afternoon. When it came time to collect our check, the bride only wanted to pay half of the amount we had agreed upon. Had we had a contract, a provision for inclement weather would have settled that rather awkward predicament. So you may need to alter or add some language to the contract to fit each situation. But once you've agreed by phone on all the particulars and filled out the contract accordingly, mail or fax two signed copies to the employer, requesting that one be returned to you with a deposit prior to the engagement. You'll be glad to have a binding contract should any problems arise.

> Always be smarter than the people who hire you.
>
> *Lena Horne*

Getting Paid

When you get paid depends on whether the gig is booked through an agent, directly by you, or through someone in the band. An agent can sometimes take up to six weeks to cut a check, while you or the bandleader usually get paid on the day of the affair or weekly if you have a house gig. As each situation is different, flexibility will be necessary, but anything longer than six weeks is unacceptable unless you were informed beforehand of special circumstances (i.e., a lengthy corporate pay schedule). A polite phone call reminder never hurts.

Organization

In order to keep track of your bookings and what money is due and from whom, you need to be organized and write everything down. It works best to coordinate your daily schedule with your work schedule to avoid any conflicts, so keep a combination day/gig planner with a daily close-up format that has lots of room for notes right by the phone. When calls come in for gigs, you can pencil in tentative dates, mark in ink the dates with signed contracts, and then plan your to-dos accordingly. You're soon to be one busy gal, and you don't want to forget who owes you what, ruin a business relationship by double booking, or overschedule yourself on gig days.

Sample Day/Gig Planner Page

❋ *Saturday, July* 9

7 A.M.	Write in diva diary
8 A.M.	Exercise: "Better than Nothing" day—take the dog for an extra long walk
9 A.M.	
10 A.M.	Practice thirty minutes; work on new song
11 A.M.	Make Mama's Veggie Beef soup for dinner
12 P.M.	
1 P.M.	Band rehearsal
2 P.M.	
3 P.M.	Go to the music store (need an extra mic cord for tonight) and pick up dress from dry cleaners
4 P.M.	Power nap!
5 P.M.	

6 P.M.   Cleansing ritual

7 P.M.   Gig—The Colony Hotel/8:30–12:30/40th birthday party/B. Duke, agent/$$

The Agent's Role

> I'm so busy, but I do have a full life. I can express myself. I'm not silent anymore.
>
> *Vanessa Carlton*

This brings me to the agent's role at the local level and how the band/agent relationship should work. A booking agent is in the business of providing all kinds of acts for weddings, company and private parties, hotels and restaurants, municipalities, and anyone else requiring live entertainment. Your band sends its promo package, which includes your picture, demo, song list, and business card to several booking agents in your area. Any interested agents will then work to find a gig or consider putting your act in an existing account that is appropriate for your band. Once a gig is found to suit, the agent will call to see if you are available for the date, to give the specifics of the occasion, and to talk money.

Negotiating a Deal with an Agent

You should never be required to pay any money up front. A legitimate agent will collect her fee for services in the form of a 15- to 20-percent commission of gross wages on the jobs she books for you. In the beginning, when you are relying on the agent's contacts and good reputation to get you gigs, you don't really have a lot of room to haggle when it comes to your gross wages. But once you've proven yourself a few times, don't be afraid to negotiate. You can usually agree on a number that's acceptable to both parties, and if the agent can't come through with a reasonable amount, walk away. It's hard to do sometimes because you want the work, but if you let an agent continuously lowball you, you'll be forever branded the "cheap band."

Play It Straight

Once the agent has gotten you a gig at a fair price, the general rule is that you hand out the agent's cards instead of your own at that particular job. It's usually done on the honor system because the

> *Some of us just go along . . . until that marvelous day people stop intimidating us—or should I say we refuse to let them intimidate us?*
>
> *Peggy Lee*

agent is not going to be checking in at every gig you do for her. I highly recommend you play it straight. A good agent has many contacts and will be advertising and pushing to book your band, especially if you've built a mutually respectful, trusting relationship.

Get References

Now, of course, there are the horror stories of the "love-ya-baby" agents who would do and say anything to book a gig and make a buck. Well, I'm sorry to say that the stories are true, so you'll need to get references from other people in the business to avoid these shysters and to find out which ones play by the book. There are usually two or three main booking agencies, depending on the size of your area, who are the most well known and widely used, so just ask the other working bands.

THE WRONG BAND FOR THE GIG

The worst situation I've ever been in was when an agent with whom we had never worked before called to book our band for a birthday party. He assured us that our style of music (adult contemporary/popular dance) was just what the client was looking for. When we pulled up to the house and saw the Harley motorcycles lined up in front, we first double-checked the address, and upon finding that we were indeed at the right house, started to have some serious reservations. Suffice it to say, we were right in our hunch that we were the wrong band for the gig. After some heavy drinking and repeated requests for "Freebird" and "Stairway to Heaven," which weren't in our repertoire, the host threatened (only half-jokingly) to throw our equipment in the pool. Some of the guests didn't look like they saw the humor, at which point we packed up at lightning speed and got the hell out of there! The sleazy agent had already gotten his deposit but claimed he couldn't get the rest of the money to pay us because we didn't finish the gig. It was one more lesson learned—in addition to always being an entertaining story to tell at dinner parties.

Self-Sabotage

You are seriously putting yourself out there now, which for some people means that it's time for a big dose of self-sabotage. The fear of success can be just as powerful a mental block as the fear of failure. I've seen it happen so many times with my voice students who are right on the verge of having a career breakthrough. Those negative voices in their heads telling them they're really not good enough or that they'll fall apart under pressure have them not showing up for an audition or canceling an appointment with an interested accompanist. I've seen extremely talented singers intentionally overbook their lives and then complain when they don't have time to even look for an opportunity to perform.

I know it's scary, so give yourself a break. But don't talk yourself out of moving forward altogether. Think of all the work you've put into this, and then find ways to help yourself ease comfortably into this next phase. For moral support, ask a good friend to accompany you to any auditions. Approach each new situation as a chapter in the adventurous and exciting book of your life. Seek guidance from one of your contacts in the music business. And keep close that feeling of joy you experience when you sing so that you'll always carry a true source of inspiration and motivation.

To Sum It Up

In this chapter, my goal is to make sure you associate the thought of auditions with words like "opportunity," "excitement," and "fun," rather than "dread," "rejection," and "failure," and it all begins with thorough preparation. Starting with the initial phone conversation with your potential employer, I show you how to sound professional and be ready for anything by knowing what questions to ask. I then guide you in picking out the best audition songs, rehearsing, and knowing when and how to give it a rest.

Thorough preparation breeds confidence, and the information I provide on interviewing your future bandmates, as well as on the role an agent plays, should give you a sense of empowerment. This, coupled with all the hard work you've done to foster your talent, will have you going to your auditions not as an inexperienced amateur begging for a job, but as a star looking for an opportunity to shine.

A DIVA NEXT DOOR SAYS
I remember when I first started playing my guitar and singing out while I was an exchange student in the Virgin Islands. I had a gig in a little tiki bar, and I made $50 a night, which I thought was the greatest. One night, I was onstage, sitting between two musicians—one was a singer, and the other was a guitar player—who were both more accomplished and experienced than me. At two different points in the evening, the singer on one side of me said, "You know, you're really more of a guitar player," and the guitar player on the other side said, "You know, you should really focus more on your singing." That was when I decided to listen to my heart and continue to do both. —Marianne

CHAPTER 9

There's No Stopping Us Now

THE INS AND OUTS OF HIGHLY SUCCESSFUL GIGGING

Now that you're with a band, please feel free to do a little victory dance. But save some energy, because there's still a lot of work to be done. Rehearsals are necessary to get you familiar with the band's repertoire and vice versa, and to give the act an overall polish before going public. You may also be asked to learn harmonies or background vocals for songs on which other band members are featured. There's much to learn about the professional and business side in order to have highly successful gigs, so here we go!

Rehearsals

Bands vary on how often they rehearse. A band that has been working together for some time may only meet once a month. For a newly formed band, however, rehearsing as much as possible before the first gig, and then dwindling down to a set schedule as you get more comfortable working with one another, makes the most sense.

Two Cardinal Rules

There are two cardinal rules for band rehearsals: don't bring visitors and come prepared. The "no visitors" rule may not seem evident, but allowing people who aren't band members to attend rehearsal is potentially awkward, distracting, or downright disastrous, and should therefore be avoided. Picture how you would feel if the bass player's girlfriend showed up and started giving her opinion on what songs you should sing or took sides in a group dispute. And even if you think your boyfriend is the greatest and would never interfere with rehearsal, his mere presence might make the other members feel shy or inhibited. It just makes for a more productive practice if band members refrain from bringing along nonmembers.

The "come prepared" rule is paramount. Believe me when I tell you that the alternative is hours of frustration and waiting around with very little progress. Being prepared for you, the lead singer, means getting a list of songs from the bandleader beforehand so that you can get familiar with the lyrics and melody at home and at your own pace. You may need to purchase a recording or the sheet music for songs that you're totally unfamiliar with. If every member comes prepared with a working knowledge of his or her respective part, then the rehearsal is the equivalent of everyone coming together, each with his own puzzle piece, and simply fitting them together. And if you're really lucky, you may even start making some beautiful music together.

Carol Welsman, two-time jazz vocalist of the year in her native Canada, certainly knows about that. She says, "Playing music in a group should be like a great conversation—everyone has something intelligent to say without being overbearing, everyone is a good listener who doesn't interrupt, and silence is never awkward."

Make Key Changes

TRICK OF THE TRADE
*A simple key change can mean the difference
between sounding mediocre and sounding great.*

At your first band rehearsal, make key changes to any songs that felt uncomfortable in your practice at home, in order to best showcase your voice. Up to this point, you've probably been doing songs in their original keys because that's the way you've always heard them on the radio and on the karaoke CDs. But there may be a better key for your particular range that makes the most use of your "sweet spot," or your strongest range of notes. Don't think you're less of a singer for changing keys. Rumor has it that even very famous pop stars lower the keys of certain songs when performing live in concert. They know how hard it is on the voice to sing at the edge of their range night after night, and so they make adjustments. You should, too. Once you've established a comfortable key, write it down next to the song on your song list, and also on your lyric sheet for future reference.

Gear Literacy

Rehearsal is the opportune time to start picking the brains of your bandmates about musical gear and function, and becoming familiar with how their particular system works. You may already understand from your experiences of sitting in at open mic nights that if you can't hear yourself sing or your voice sounds like it's being amplified in a tin can, no amount of practice is going to allow you to sing or sound your best. Armed with some basic knowledge, however, you can communicate your sound equipment needs. Begin by asking questions that are directly related to your purposes as a vocalist, like where to plug in your microphone, and basics of the band's P.A. system, etc., and going from there as time goes on. Your bandmates will appreciate having a vocalist they can effectively communicate with.

Another Word (or Two) from Mark Widick, M.D.

You've worked so hard to get your voice in the best shape possible, and you need to know how to keep it that way now that you're rehearsing and performing with a band—a band that's more than likely a lot louder than your karaoke machine at home. I asked for Dr. Mark Widick's advice once again, this time to explain how an entertainer can avoid wear and tear and maintain a healthy singing voice. Here's what he had to say:

> Numbers one, two, and three on the list for keeping a healthy voice are the use of proper amplification and monitors in practice and performance. Don't try for even five minutes to sing over a band without a microphone plugged into an amplification system that includes your own personal monitor. You will strain your voice and over time possibly develop serious throat problems. Also, make sure that you warm-up sufficiently before you begin singing, and at the end of your performance, choose less demanding songs as a sort of warm down.
>
> Another critical aspect of singing is the ability to hear well. Loud noise such as amplified music causes hearing loss, so you need to protect yourself by never standing directly in front of a speaker and by wearing earplugs whenever possible. Musician earplugs are available which reduce volume levels evenly, allowing the musician to accurately monitor sound at a reduced volume. Get a hearing test and keep a copy of the results, and then retest periodically to determine if you are suffering any hearing loss.

Gigs

Once you've agreed to do a gig—even if it's only by word of mouth with the bandleader—you should honor your commitment. A practice that some singers have been known to do is to make up a phony excuse and renege on a gig when a better paying opportunity comes along. You may make some extra money that one time, but in the long run, you'll lose out. No one is going to keep calling you if they can't trust that you'll do what you say you're going to do.

Ideal Preparation

On the day of your gig, follow these tips for the ideal preparation to put you in good singing voice and give you high energy for the evening. (This is ideal, but I know near impossible for most—just do your best.)

* Get plenty of sleep the night before.
* Do your normal twenty-minute vocal warm-up in the morning, and then go out and get some exercise. It's not the day to schedule the triathlon, but the Ultimate Diva Workout from chapter 4 will give you energy for the rest of the day and night.
* Make a conscious effort not to talk overly much during the day.
* In the late afternoon, take a twenty-minute power nap. You'll probably be up late, so treat yourself to the luxury.
* An hour or so before you leave for the gig, eat a light meal that includes both carbohydrates and protein. (For something fast, easy, and healthy, I swear by a tuna fish or chicken salad sandwich with lettuce and tomato.) Be sure to give yourself plenty of time to digest your meal before you perform, because not only is burping unattractive on the mic (duh), but the energy needed for digestion can slow you down and be a hindrance to singing.
* Check your gig bag to make sure you have packed everything you'll need. It's always a good idea to include a bottle of water, a small snack, and a little makeup bag for touch ups.
* Finally, do a five-minute warm-up again before you leave home, preferably as a part of the cleansing ritual described in chapter 8. The steam is wonderful for hydrating your pipes and opening up nasal passages, not to mention giving your face a nice rosy glow. (This is the diva's idea of multitasking.)

As tempted as you may be to get one last bit of practice in, resist and stay quiet. The engine and traffic noise will cause you to sing louder than normal to hear yourself, and this could possibly strain your voice before you even take the stage.

Natural and Home Remedies for a Hoarse Voice

If your voice is at all hoarse from overuse, try one of these natural or home remedies I've used and that I've heard various singers swear by:

* Licorice tea with honey
* Throat Coat herbal tea (found in health-food stores)
* Fisherman's Friend lozenges
* Pickled ginger
* Salty potato chips
* Sea salt and water gargle
* Mildly hot peppers
* Hard candy
* Chips and salsa

Setup and Breakdown

With gig bag, mic, and music stand in hand, and wearing an outfit that screams "diva" (better to be overdressed than underdressed), arrive at least one hour before showtime, unless otherwise instructed.

TRICK OF THE TRADE
Wear comfortable clothes and shoes to the gig so you can help with setup and breakdown.

You'll keep your stage clothes from getting messed up, your feet will thank you, and you'll earn enormous gratitude and respect from your band. A house band can often leave the heaviest equipment set up on its off nights, but it is required to tidy up the stage area by rolling cords and putting away smaller items like stands. If this is the case, still be prepared to pitch in after the gig, but rather than change (by the time you finish changing clothes, the work will be done), just bring a pair of comfortable shoes. I keep a pair of black ballet slippers in my gig bag at all times, just in case. They're light-weight, comfy, don't take up much space, and they look prettier with my outfits than a pair of sneakers—a diva until the bitter end.

Sound Check

After getting your mic plugged in and your stands in place with your songbook easily accessible, conduct a sound check with the band. Basically this involves partially running through a song and making sure that you can hear yourself sing over the music without straining and without feedback. Feedback is a loud, piercing squeal that can emit from speakers or a distortion that makes the voice sound abnormal. You also want to make sure your voice is featured in the most complimentary way, so remember this phrase: "How about a little more reverb?"

TRICK OF THE TRADE
Reverb, one of a singer's dearest friends, is an effect on most mixing boards that when applied to the vocal channel, gives the voice a slight echo, which in turn pleasantly fills out the sound.

Hopefully you will have already worked out the best setting for your voice in rehearsal, so it will only be a matter of making minor adjustments in sound check.

Making Set Lists

After sound check, the bandleader may want to get with you before you're on to come up with set lists for the gig. When you're giving your input, rather than randomly naming songs from your repertoire, consider the fact that every gig is a different type of occasion or venue. There are certain ballads, for instance, which would be more suitable for a particular audience than others. If it's going to be a younger crowd, I suggest something like Nora Jones's "Don't Know Why" instead of an old standard like "The Very Thought of You," because they are more likely to recognize and enjoy the former.

Also keep in mind that the music should flow with your time frame, building in volume and tempo as the gig progresses. The first set list should contain more of your slow- to medium-tempo tunes, with maybe an upbeat song right before the break as a teaser of what's to come. Also, you'll want the first few songs you sing to be some of your easier ones so that you can warm up a bit before tackling the more challenging numbers. The second set should mix up medium- and fast-tempo songs, and the last set or two should be mostly high-energy songs with a couple of ballads thrown in. Of course, this is a general strategy for showcasing your music in the most flattering and effective way, but it usually works very well. Some of the more experienced bandleaders don't use set lists, preferring instead to watch the crowd and spontaneously call songs, but should you be asked, at least you'll have a better idea of what songs in your repertoire would work best for each set.

Lighting

By no stretch of the imagination am I an expert on lighting, but I do know that it is one of the most overlooked aspects of a performance. It doesn't matter how tight and talented you and your band are, if the establishment sticks you in a dark corner, you will most likely get a lukewarm response, and you will definitely lack the "wow" factor. Spotlights make it possible for the audience to see you better, obviously, but they also work on a psychological level by establishing your group as an act worth watching.

In the event that a venue doesn't have a lighting rig over the stage, or a stage for that matter, a band should always carry its own lights to establish its performance space. Ask the bandleader if the band has any, and if not, offer to pitch in to buy at least one rack of lights. Karaoke stores and the DJ sections of music stores usually have reasonably priced starter kits.

TRICK OF THE TRADE
If you want to further enhance the lighting for your performances, purchase gels.

Gels are colored transparencies that can be fitted over a stage light for different effects. They come in a variety of colors, and you can match them to the mood of a particular gig or to the style of your band's music. Lavender and blue gels work well for a jazz and blues band, and red and amber gels give a dance band a high-energy feel.

Performing

Once you've taken the stage to perform, there are some basic rules of conduct. Before you begin singing, take the microphone off the mic stand and place the stand behind you. This is an old-school rule, but one that gives you more mobility and control than leaving the mic on the stand and standing in front of it. I recently saw a seasoned performer who held her mic (good), but left the stand in front of her (bad). For much of the performance, the stand annoyingly obscured my view of her.

No Sitting on the Job

Also, sitting on a stool all night while you perform diminishes your physical ability to sing, lessens the visual impact of your performance, and shows a certain disregard for the profession. There may be rare instances when sitting down on the job is acceptable, like if you are providing the background music for a restaurant, or occasionally while you're singing a ballad. But if someone is paying you to perform onstage, you need to be working it, diva. How is the crowd going to be inspired to get excited about your music or to dance if you can't even summon up the energy to stand? Rest your feet when you get home.

THE FOOL ON THE STOOL

Not too long ago, my band had a private gig, and we were able to get out of our steady gig for the night. The manager hired another band to replace us with the thought that if they worked out, they could fill in for us on any future dates. Well, did I get an earful from the manager when we returned. Apparently the replacement band played the right kind of music and the female vocalist sang well, but she planted herself on a stool the whole night with a bored look on her face, even while singing the up-tempo dance music! The manager said that he received several complaints and that he definitely wouldn't have that band back to his club.

Always Appear in Control

You want to always appear to your audience that you're in control, professional, and having a good time. So, when communicating with other band members onstage, even if it's to say that you can't hear yourself in the mix because the damn guitar player is too loud again, wear a smile.

Or say you are drawing a blank on your lyrics in the middle of a song that you thought you knew. I've gotten pretty good at making up my own words since that wedding where I made up the "peanut-butter-and-jelly" lyric, and no one but the band seems to notice. You can always resort to repeating the verse you do remember, or asking the closest band member (with a big smile, of course) if they can help you out. The audience will think that you're at ease, perhaps sharing a little inside joke, and having fun, even when there are complications.

Patter

> **GOLDEN RULE**
> *Don't forget to say "thank you" when you receive applause.*

Sometimes performers make the mistake of not showing their gratitude. Perhaps they are preoccupied with thinking of the next song, or they may not think the acknowledgment is that important. Wrong! Great entertainment is always interactive.

Start with a "thank you," and as you get more comfortable talking to the crowd, expand on your in-between-songs banter, or patter. For example, every once in awhile you can give a brief history of the song you are going to sing, or tell the audience how lovely they are and what a fantastic time you are having performing for them. Sometimes with an especially rowdy crowd, the best approach is to ask that classic question, "Is everyone having a good time?" (Only ask this if they obviously are, and you know the answer will be "Yeah!") The key is to talk just enough for the audience to identify with you, but not to the extent of being intrusive or obnoxious—and not overly much when the dance floor is full. I worked with a guy (only once) who told longwinded stories and bad jokes between every other song, and it was a wedding, no less. It was like being a part of a really bad cabaret act. The bride was obviously distraught, but he didn't seem to notice her reaction or that of her guests as they steadily left the dance floor to hang out at the bar in the other room.

Have Fun

Your first gig will reveal obvious areas of strength and weakness. During breaks, take notes of any problems so you'll remember to work on them at home or at your next band rehearsal. But don't obsess over mistakes during the performance. It will only affect you negatively, and the truth is, you may well be the only person who notices. At most parties, weddings, or clubs, your audience will be

more interested in talking, eating, drinking, and dancing than in critiquing every little detail of the band. As long as you can do most of
the requests, stay concentrated on adding the right ambience for the
occasion, and schmooze a little with your audience, you'll be a big
hit. Most importantly, have fun! You are finally doing what you've
always dreamed of, so live in the moment, and try to enjoy your
debut; it will only happen once.

Work the Crowd

GOLDEN RULE
Schmoozing is essential.

Just what is schmoozing, you ask? Well, schmoozing is about building relationships with your audience. It means taking time on your
breaks to say "hello" and to show your appreciation for their support.
It's as easy as complimenting the way someone is dressed, graciously
taking a song request, or simply making eye contact and giving
someone a smile. Nothing endears an audience to a performer
faster, so work that crowd onstage and during the breaks.

Don't Miss a Photo Op

TRICK OF THE TRADE
*Always have a camera handy at gigs
in the event of a photo op.*

As silly as it may seem, a few pictures of you and your band with a
politician, local celebrity, or a big-time star that happens into the
establishment where you are performing can make people stop and
take notice. Use them on the band's Web site if you have one, or use
them in your promotional material. Attach the latest picture to your

e-mails announcing an upcoming gig. These kinds of pictures are truly worth a thousand words when you consider how effective they are in raising your band's status in the eyes of your existing fans and capturing the attention of new fans.

Food

Occasionally, the party or establishment for whom you're performing will invite the band to eat and drink. This is a wonderful bonus, but it should never be assumed as a given. I heard of one local singer whose appetite was legendary. Once at a dinner party where she was performing, she actually grabbed a handful of crab puffs off of a passing waiter's tray while she was onstage singing. Then she proceeded to take nibbles in between songs! First of all, eating onstage is so obviously wrong, I won't even comment. Second, if you weren't told beforehand that a meal would be provided, eat before the gig or bring a snack in your bag to eat on break.

TASTY TIDBIT
For a convenient and nutritionally balanced snack to get you through a gig, eat an energy bar.

Drink

And so we come to the alcoholic beverages that are readily available at most gigs. Please use caution while drinking and operating a microphone! When I started performing, I used to rely on a glass of wine to loosen me up and help with my nerves. But I found that even one glass can dehydrate your vocal cords and give you "dry throat." The detrimental effect on my voice far outweighed any benefits. And, of course, there are the obvious consequences of two or more drinks. After consuming a few toddies, you'll probably think you are giving the performance of a lifetime, but I can assure you it won't be the kind of performance you'll want to be remembered for.

A wonderful singer around town, whom we'll call "Anna," learned this lesson early on in her career. Anna was performing at a wedding reception and was offered champagne with which to toast the bride and groom. As Anna hadn't had much experience with the effects of champagne, she was happy to accept that one, and then another glass, and yet another glass when the host insisted. And although later that evening, most of the men at the party appreciated her impersonation of Marilyn Monroe, dress blowing up over her head as she stood astride a floor fan, the bride was none too pleased.

Dealing with the Obnoxious

I hate to mention it, but there will be times when audience members get out of hand. Wedding receptions are especially ripe for bad behavior, due to the usual offering of an open bar. If you find that ignoring a heckler or brushing off a caustic patron isn't working, and you're having a difficult time doing your job because of them, don't try to handle it yourself. The crowd probably won't know what has caused you to start berating one of its own, and the whole bunch of them could very well turn on you. Tell the offender to speak to the manager, or if that fails to alleviate the problem, take a break and go inform the manager yourself. It puts you out of the loop so you can continue performing your diva duties.

SET LIMITS

Of course, this only works if there is a manager available. I once did a holiday company party at a private home hosted by the couple who owned the business. It started out fine—they had a beautiful grand piano, the acoustics in the living room where we were set up sounded great, and everyone seemed to be enjoying themselves. Fast-forward to two hours later, and the hostess with the mostess decided to show off her new boob job to the band. We all said our congratulations, but it didn't stop there. By the last set, the atmosphere had turned from festive to frenzied as some of the guests followed their hostess's lead and started getting in various stages of undress. When the lady of the house smacked my backside as she passed by, I knew I was in the middle of a midlife crisis gone haywire, and I wanted out fast! We all packed up then and there. The moral of the story: Set limits when dealing with obnoxious audience members—no one expects you to take abuse.

Public Relations

PRACTICAL GEM
Always tip the bartender.

Just think of tipping the bartender as paying your public-relations department. The bartender is the person, more times than not, who patrons converse with about the comings and goings of an establishment or party—including talk of how good (or bad) the band is. Even if the drinks are on the house or all you order is a glass of water, throw the bartender a small tip. You'll have made a big fan who'll be much more likely to sing your praises to anyone who'll listen.

Nerves

Finally, remember this if nerves threaten to get the best of you: You've worked hard to get where you are, and you deserve to be there. The audience already assumes you're a qualified professional by virtue of the fact that you're the one who is front and center on the stage. So prove them right! Use that extra adrenaline to your advantage to heighten the energy of your performance. Or refer back to the stage fright section in chapter 6 for some calming exercises.

> I get nervous when I don't get nervous. If I'm nervous, I know I'm going to have a good show.
>
> *Beyonce Knowles*

Special Gigs

Every gig has variations from another to which you can usually adapt sufficiently once you get there. For instance, you may show up at a gig and find out that the establishment is expecting a big party of forty-somethings, so you make your set lists accordingly, concentrating on songs from the sixties to the present. But there are a few kinds of gigs that require a different approach and/or some special attention.

Weddings

Wedding receptions are usually the best-paying private parties, so if you want plenty of referrals, follow my advice. First of all, make a conscious effort not to upstage the bride in any way. This is her big day after all, so don't wear white, and don't wear anything too revealing.

> I never reveal too much of my sexuality. I give a little taste, but I don't give it all.
> *Queen Latifah*

The stress level for the bride and groom will be high, because they are usually trying to accommodate and please everyone. In order to relieve some of the strain of their responsibilities, mail them a Wedding Reception Information Sheet (see appendix D) for them to complete and return to you before the big day. The purpose of the information sheet is to ascertain all the particulars of the reception—like the first dance choice and the name of the best man giving the toast, for example—so that the day runs smoothly. With this completed sheet in hand, you can coordinate with the caterer or the banquet manager beforehand so that everyone is on the same page. It will also prepare you for announcements with a list of the names of each person in the wedding party, as well as their relationships to the bride and groom and their special roles for the day. Most importantly, you'll be able to personalize the announcements and make it appear to the wedding party and guests that this is indeed a very special occasion, and not the eighth wedding reception you've done that month.

Club Dates

A club date, or as some call it, a casual or a one-nighter, is a gig, usually a private party, in which you are called to perform with a band that you don't regularly perform with. Many singers shy away from this type of situation because it isn't rehearsed. I'll give you some tips on how to get through a club date with ease so you won't hesitate to take advantage of these lucrative opportunities.

First, you need to show up on time, dressed to impress, with your own microphone and mic stand. Next, have a well-organized song list for yourself and a few extra copies to hand out to the bandleader and possibly the guitar or keyboard player. The songs should be categorized by style, such as ballad, swing, Top Forty, etc., with your keys for each song clearly marked. The bandleader will then be able to easily find what he's looking for in order to call songs.

> We cannot direct the wind, but we can adjust the sails.
> *Dolly Parton*

During the gig, pay attention to the bandleader at all times. He may have to ask you to call a song if he's involved and can't study your song list himself. For instance, say the band is playing a disco number and the dance floor is full. The bandleader will probably want to do another disco song since it is obviously working well with the crowd. Be ready to call a similar song so he doesn't have to stop the music (thus interrupting the mood) but rather can signal the band to the key change, and flow right into your song.

New Year's Eve Gigs

I think it's worth mentioning here the mother of all gigs, New Year's Eve. This will probably be your best-paying job all year, so it deserves a little extra attention. Most every establishment, public and private, as well as municipalities and many private homeowners, are going to hire live entertainment to bring in the new year. There are so many opportunities for work on this night that it is often said you have to be a pretty bad musician or vocalist if you aren't working on New Year's Eve.

The phone usually starts ringing around June with inquiries about availability and price. Hold out for a while, and don't make any decisions for another couple of months. However, don't get greedy and hold out for better offers too long, say past September, or you may end up jobless on New Year's Eve. How embarrassed will you be?

AULD LANG SYNE

Oh, by the way, make sure you learn all the words to "Auld Lang Syne." My first New Year's Eve gig, it didn't even occur to me to have these lyrics handy; I had always just "la-la'd" my way through the song at past celebrations I'd attended. It was only at the stroke of midnight that I realized I had a problem. I stood on the stage with everyone looking at me and rather awkwardly tried to read lips and fake my way through the verses. Learn it.

To Sum It Up

There are so many variables in performing, and because of this, I can't give you advice for every situation. But in this chapter I have told you how to prepare at home so as to be in the best voice possible, how to set up and do a sound check for a comfortable performance, and the most important rules of behavior during a gig. By keeping this high level of profession-

> "
> How do you explain what it feels like to get on the stage and make poetry that you know sinks into the hearts and souls of people who are unable to express it?
> *Nina Simone*
> "

alism, you should be able to go anywhere, handle anything that's thrown at you, and make a stunning impression wherever you perform. One of the best days of my life was the first time I got paid for singing. It seemed too good to be true that doing something I loved could actually be lucrative, that work could feel like play. But it was and continues to be true, and my hope as of this chapter is that you, too, are experiencing the joys of divahood.

A DIVA NEXT DOOR SAYS

I've found that if you are in a concert situation where a sound company is provided—the "sound men," as they are referred to—will be the most important people you interact with (besides the audience, of course). They can either make or break your performance because they are responsible for handling your sound onstage and the feed to the audience, etc. I can't emphasize enough the importance of being pleasant, understanding, patient, and friendly. I've seen other performers approach the sound men with demanding, know-it-all tones, which got them nowhere—and it showed! Keep in mind that the sound crew has a hard job. They have to deal with getting the right sound for the performer, technical issues, remaining on schedule, and dealing with unexpected problems and changes, all in a high-pressure situation. They are the glue that really holds a show together, so treat them with respect, and the difference will show in your show. —Jamie

CHAPTER 10

Born to Fly

EXPANDING YOUR HORIZONS

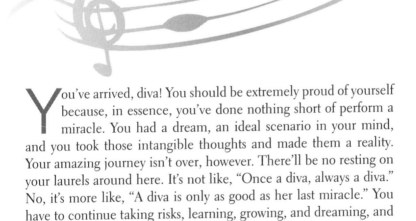

Y ou've arrived, diva! You should be extremely proud of yourself because, in essence, you've done nothing short of perform a miracle. You had a dream, an ideal scenario in your mind, and you took those intangible thoughts and made them a reality. Your amazing journey isn't over, however. There'll be no resting on your laurels around here. It's not like, "Once a diva, always a diva." No, it's more like, "A diva is only as good as her last miracle." You have to continue taking risks, learning, growing, and dreaming, and by following just three simple rules, you'll never have any problem keeping your hard-earned title.

GOLDEN RULE: THREE RULES FOR THE DIVA TO RULE

❖ Think of each gig as an audition
❖ Continue improving your craft
❖ Take it to the next level

Think of Each Gig As an Audition

Think back now to when you went on your first auditions. Remember how you felt the excitement and wonder of just being there, and the desire to do your absolute best? Remember your gratitude when you got the job, and your amazement that you were actually going to get paid for singing? Reflect upon the joy that you provide others when you make a day or an occasion special with your unique talent. That attitude is what you need to carry with you to each gig, not only because it is good for your soul, but because it is good for your business.

The Domino Effect

Every audience is full of potential clients and opportunities for future work. If you consistently give 100 percent, no matter the venue or the size of the audience, you'll never have to spend a dime on advertising or worry about job security because of the "domino effect." Here's what I mean: Mr. and Mrs. Smith see you performing in a lounge and ask you to entertain at their upcoming anniversary party at the country club. While you're performing at their party, a guest asks if you'll sing the demo of his original song, and the manager of the country club wants a card so he can call you about doing the holiday dinner dance. The producer at the studio where you sing the demo is impressed with your talent and professionalism and is interested in hiring you for future sessions . . .

> " I guess when people come to see me, they know they're going to get 150 percent. It's been that way ever since I stepped out on stage for the first time."
>
> *Patti LaBelle*

One local singer who embodies this diva principle was singing to five people on a Sunday afternoon at her weekly tiki bar gig. Two of the people happened to be German music producers on vacation, and they liked what they heard—so much so that they flew her to Germany to record two pop songs for one of their projects, and she earned a hefty check. Never in a million years did she think that her tiki bar gig would result in a free trip to Europe and more money than she'd ever earned at one time. But because she continues to approach her work in true diva fashion, I'm positive that won't be her last surprising windfall. This is how the "domino effect" works, and why you should think of each gig as an audition.

> All I ever intended was to make a living at what I do. Everything I've achieved since then is above and beyond.
>
> *Shania Twain*

Continue Improving Your Craft

Now let's take a glimpse at what it looks like when a singer fails to hold on to that initial enthusiasm. I've witnessed it many times when going out to see live entertainment. She performs adequately, but she looks at her watch too much, often sits on a stool, and gives the impression that she's on autopilot and would rather be somewhere else. If you were to talk to her, you'd find that she considers her current gig nothing but a paycheck, merely a stepping-stone for bigger and better things.

I'll be the first to admit that once you've been a professional vocalist for awhile, it becomes a job like any other, with good days and bad. But the challenge, not just in singing, but in life, is to keep rediscovering the joy. To make sure that the proverbial fire doesn't go out in your singing career, you need to reignite the flame by continuing to improve your craft.

Update Your Repertoire Regularly

The easiest and most immediate way to stay fresh is to keep your repertoire updated. Any professional vocalist or musician will tell you that new songs are like a shot of adrenaline to a band. Learning just a few songs every month or so will keep you sounding current and feeling excited about performing.

PRACTICAL GEM

The soundtracks from popular movies are a great source for material. Movie soundtracks often have classic songs that are appealing to all age groups, as well as the latest hits to keep you sounding hip to your younger audience members.

And if you are the house band, regularly learning new material is mandatory. There will always be a honeymoon period when the staff is thrilled to hear the new band's sound. But it won't take long for them to get sick of the same old songs played week after week. They'll soon be grumbling about the band to the manager or possibly the customers, and the next thing you know, your popularity will have plummeted. I would strongly suggest that in addition to learning new songs regularly, from time to time you even learn some of the staff members' song requests to keep them happy and on your side. Announce on the microphone that you've learned a new song and dedicate it to the staff member who requested it—talk about promoting good morale in your workplace.

> You've got to continue to grow, or you're just like last night's cornbread— stale and dry.
>
> *Loretta Lynn*

Videotape Your Act

Just as recording yourself sing for the first time is an enlightening and educational experience, so is videotaping your performance. You may find that you don't move around enough to make for a visually exciting show. Or maybe you unconsciously repeat one gesture over and over or keep your eyes closed all the time—two of the most obvious signs of a novice. By watching my first videotaped performance, I realized that I made a funny face every time I missed a note or forgot a word. The lesson learned was that my little mistakes were barely noticeable until I called attention to them by making funny faces. By watching yourself on tape, you can clearly see the areas that need attention.

Once you've done a dry run for your educational purposes, consider having someone videotape your act for promotional purposes. More and more, agents and clients want a video of the band they're considering to hire instead of the traditional audio CD and a photo. Having a video demo gives you one more promotional tool with which to sell your act.

See Live Music

You should continue going to see live music whenever possible for several reasons. First, it's plain good karma to support your fellow musicians and live music in your community. Also, watching other vocalists perform can inspire you to learn new material, improve upon your existing repertoire, and try some different moves. And as any good businessperson knows, to stay on the cutting edge, you must check out your direct competition from time to time to see what is working for them.

And whenever you see a band that is similar in style and quality, try to establish a relationship in which you recommend each other for gigs when one or the other of you is unavailable. This is a smart business move all around. You'll make your clients happy even if they call you for a gig and you're unavailable, because you can refer them to a good replacement band. And when it works both ways, you'll be getting gig referrals from yet another source.

Discover New Inspiration

Whenever you find yourself unmotivated to practice or learn new songs, or you're feeling a general malaise about singing, you need to take a good shot of inspiration by going to the record store or a concert to discover a new vocalist. I've found this to be one of the best remedies for the diva blues. To come upon a beautiful, fresh voice that you've never heard before is like taking a musical Prozac.

When you're choosing a CD or a concert to attend, be impulsive, and don't question what you're drawn to. Maybe the cover jumps out at you, or the song titles on a CD are intriguing, or a flyer for a concert catches your eye. I always try to go with my initial impulse, and it has worked time after time. Using this technique, I discovered the sublime Alison Krauss, Diana Krall, and Shawn Colvin long before their huge commercial success—upon listening to each of these women for the first time, I felt like freakin' Christopher Columbus! I've discovered divas who have yet to become a household name, who are a household name in another country or in a genre I'm not as familiar with, or who were at one time a household name and I just had a gap in my diva education. Whatever the case may be, there is a legion of divas in every musical style from years past to present who are out there just waiting to inspire you, too.

My Favorite Diva Discoveries

* ❄ Ann Hampton Callaway
* ❄ Blossom Dearie
* ❄ Carol Welsman
* ❄ Eydie Gorme
* ❄ Keely Smith
* ❄ Lisa Ekdahl
* ❄ Neena Freelon
* ❄ Noa
* ❄ Patricia Cathcart Andress of Tuck and Patty
* ❄ Stacey Kent

> " I was always a singer and a dancer, and I always wanted to be an actress. For me, it's all just one thing.
> *Jennifer Lopez* "

A Triple Threat

Become a "triple threat" by taking acting and dance classes. You can use elements of both to make your performances even more engaging and exciting. Dance helps you to become more comfortable with your body and movement, and even helps you hear music in a whole new way. A great drummer I know mentioned that he took tap dancing lessons for years and that it had helped him in learning even the most intricate rhythms on the drums. Guess who is currently taking a tap class? Once a week, I'm getting a great workout and enhancing my sense of rhythm. And who knows—maybe I'll eventually work a little soft-shoe into the act.

> Good singing is a form of good acting.
> *Judy Garland*

Put acting lessons at the top of your to-do list, because a vocalist is really an actor whose lines are sung rather than spoken. Acting lessons can help to get you over any lingering shyness and to draw you completely out of your shell. Nothing brings an audience to their feet faster than a performer who is uninhibited and fearless. And remember the final song-mastery step of giving every song a soul injection? Acting lessons can introduce you to different techniques for finding inspiration and expressing emotion to better achieve this.

Learn Another Language

If you've ever heard Celine Dion sing in French or Linda Ronstadt sing in Spanish, you already know how another language can take a song and a singer to new heights. And if you want your audience to fall to their knees, familiarize yourself with a foreign language.

> I'm such a chameleon. I never get bored.
> *Natalie Imbruglia*

Brush up on one of the Romance languages like French, Spanish, or Italian to sing a classic love song, a well-known standard, or a hot new Latin pop song. It's not even necessary that you speak the language fluently. As long as you learn how to pronounce the words properly, you can convincingly sing a foreign-language song. Ask someone you know who speaks the language of a song you want to learn to write out the words phonetically. This just adds to your value as a performer and may lead to more opportunities in the studio as well.

Mentor Others

A sure way to improve your craft is to mentor other gals who want to join the diva ranks. A few years into my career, a woman approached me at a gig and inquired about voice lessons. Although I was flattered, I declined because with only three or so years under my belt, I didn't feel like much of an authority. She was persistent, however, so I agreed to teach her as much as I could, and then send her on her way to find a more experienced teacher. Well, I was pleasantly surprised at how much I actually did have to offer, and even more surprised by how much I myself learned in the process.

"Inspiration is a circular thing." Those were the words of diva extraordinaire, Ann Hampton Callaway, the Tony award®–nominated singer and songwriter, to Barbra Streisand, who regularly takes time out of her hectic world-touring schedule to teach master classes and work with other singers.

Get Away

Now that your play has become your work, you may feel inclined to keep going and going like the Energizer bunny. Taking an extended vacation from something you love doing may seem unnecessary, frivolous, and a highly unlikely way to continue improving your craft. But there is nothing quite as refreshing and motivating as getting away from your passion from time to time. You'll be amazed at how even a brief respite can restore energy you were probably too busy to notice was missing, and can spur you toward a giant leap of growth. I've had this experience too many times to discount it or to encourage you not to do the same.

I recommend that you get away entirely from all things musical; take a mental and physical departure for at least a week if you can swing it. That may entail lying by the pool or on the beach with a trashy novel (wearing sunscreen, of course), exploring the antique district and art museums in a quaint neighboring town, or taking a long overdue trip to visit good friends—whatever sounds fun, stress-free, and relaxing to you. It's the whole "absence-makes-the-heart-grow-fonder" phenomenon. You'll return to performing with a whole new appreciation and outlook, the sparks will fly, and that's when momentous changes occur.

Take It to the Next Level

You have put an enormous amount of time and energy into becoming a diva, and you're continuing to learn and grow, but why stop now? Taking your career to the next level is the only place to go. If you find yourself wanting more control over the way the gigs are run and the way the business is handled, start your own band. Once you know the musicians, have a feel for your local market, and are familiar with the movers and shakers around town, there's no reason you shouldn't be at the helm.

Music Theory

It only makes sense that at some point you are going to want a better understanding of music—it is now your vocation, after all. There are so many ways that learning some basic music theory is beneficial, not the least of which is the ability to speak the language of music so you can communicate more effectively with band members. Enroll in a basic theory class at a community college, or teach yourself with a beginner's instructional book. If you can find a sight-reading course in your area, this would be very helpful, especially if you want to get recording studio work. And probably the most advantageous approach to learning music for the long run is to pick up an instrument with which you can eventually accompany yourself, like the guitar or piano. Your local music store probably has teachers on staff, or they can recommend a private teacher.

> "Walking into a guitar store was almost an act of courage. They would look you up and down and say, "Hi, honey, are you here to get something for your boyfriend?"
>
> *Ani DiFranco*

Make a CD to Sell

Consider recording a CD of your most-requested songs to sell at gigs. The initial investment is a bit pricey when you take into account the cost of the recording studio, mechanical licensing fees, artwork or photographs, and CD duplication. But this venture can be a huge learning experience and eventually quite profitable, especially for bands with a large following.

Once you are firm on the date that your finished CDs will be shipped to you from the manufacturing company, plan a "CD release party." All this means is that you create an event for all of those fans on your mailing list, friends, and family members to come and celebrate (and hopefully buy) your new CD. If you're a house band, the manager of the club will probably be thrilled to host a party in your honor on an off night. And even if you don't have a steady gig somewhere, approach a club where you would like to work with the idea. It's hard to turn down an offer of free music for the night along with a guaranteed crowd.

In the Studio

Once in a professional recording studio for this project or any other, you want to look and sound like you know what you're doing, not only for the sake of a great outcome on the recording, but also to increase your chances of getting called back to the studio for other work. If you're paying for the studio time on your own project, you and your band have complete control. But if you're hired to sing a commercial jingle or a demo, the producer is in charge. Let me reiterate this important point because it is the biggest mistake that session singers make: Excluding your own projects on which you're footing the bill, take direction and just sing unless someone asks for your opinion. A sure way to never get called back to a studio is to tell the producer the way you think things should be done. Once you've been working at a studio and built a relationship with the producer, over time you may be asked for your input. But until then, be quiet unless singing.

THE PRODUCER

To show you what you are expected to sing on the project, the producer will provide a chart, or demonstrate by either singing the melody or playing it on a piano. I don't sight-read very well, so I'll always ask the producer to go over the melody with me a couple of times to reinforce what is needed. Time is money in the studio, so if you want to be called back for future work, be a quick study.

THE ENGINEER

Next you'll go into the vocal booth and put on headphones, or "the cans," as they're sometimes referred to. The engineer is the person at the mixing board, and her job at this point is to make sure you have a comfortable mix of the music and your voice in your headphones.

TRICK OF THE TRADE

Once you're happy with the mix and before you start recording, slide one side of the headphones off your ear.

Though you would think it'd be easier to stay in tune in the studio where you have a controlled, quiet environment (unlike in live performances), for most people it's much harder. Sliding one headphone off so that you're hearing your voice through the cans and live in the room helps you to avoid any pitch problems.

AGAIN, WITH FEELING

When you start recording, you're going to have to enunciate your words and sing with great feeling. It may feel as if you're overdoing it, but for some reason, it takes this extra energy to be able to understand what you are singing and for the feeling to come across on a recording. The voice will sound lifeless, otherwise. And for jingle singing, when you're trying to sell a product or a service, it is especially important.

TRICK OF THE TRADE

A sure way to convey enthusiasm on a recording is to smile when you sing.

Really, you can almost hear a smile. So even though you are concentrating on reading the lyrics and singing the melody correctly, you need to remember to smile when you sing a happy song. Many times when singing jingles, I've even taped a "smile" sign to the music stand to remind me.

Give Back

Giving something back to your community in the way of donating live music for a charitable event is like opening up a huge can of gummi worms. While writing out a check is all well and good, when you can give your time and talent to a worthy cause, all seems right in the world. The organization is thrilled because they don't have to fork out the dough to set the right musical mood for the affair (very important for making attendees feel generous and giving), you're happy to be doing something you love in a way that will serve others, and even though it is with the most altruistic intentions, the deed generates good press and wonderful contacts that are great for your business. Choose a cause or an organization that you feel strongly about, make a call, and get ready for your cup to runneth over.

Songwriting

Maybe you have some original song ideas and want to explore songwriting. Go for it! For many singers and musicians, this is a natural progression. Ask the members of your band if they are interested in getting together once a week to collaborate on original material. Or use those college and music store bulletin boards again to find a songwriting partner. The Internet is a helpful source for finding songwriting associations in your area that meet regularly to provide education and support, and to connect like-minded collaborators. And there are many Web sites for songwriters across the country,

including the Muse's Muse (*www.musesmuse.com*) and the Songwriter's Tip Jar (*www.songwriterstipjar.com*).

THE PROCESS

Songwriting is a process, just like learning how to be a professional
singer is a process. It takes patience, study, repetition, and dedication. Diane Warren, perhaps the most prolific songwriter in pop
music today, wrote for a decade before even breaking into the business. Grammy Award®–winning singer/songwriter Shawn Colvin
honed her craft for years in small clubs before landing her first
record deal. The point is that it's highly unlikely that you'll wake up
one morning, decide you want to write songs, and produce a hit on
the first go. Nevertheless, the process of songwriting can be very
rewarding in and of itself.

COMMERCIAL JINGLES

One way to polish your songwriting skills, and perhaps make some
money in the process, is to seek "work-for-hire" opportunities in your
area. "Work-for-hire" means you get paid a one-time fee to write a
song for a specific purpose, like a commercial jingle, for example.
There are a few approaches in getting your foot in the door of this
niche. You could try to go straight to the individual businesses, or
call on the advertising agencies in town. Or if you've already made
some contacts at a recording studio when you recorded your demo
or your CD, use them. Recording studios usually work with advertising agencies, or directly with businesses wanting to advertise, in
developing catchy theme songs for TV and radio. I broke into the
jingle business by writing a jingle with the keyboard player in my
band for a fictitious coffee house. I dropped it off in person to the
two recording studios in town where I already had contacts, along
with a short bio and a cover letter that stated my desire to write
and/or sing jingles. Try it and see what happens.

COPYRIGHT REGISTRATION

For a work-for-hire creation, the person or company that commis-
sions the work-for-hire project retains the copyright. For your personal projects, however, you should protect your composition from

unauthorized use. Do this once you've finished writing a song, but before you perform it in public or send out a recording. This is easily done through the Library of Congress. You simply fill out a Form PA, which you can get online (*www.copyright.gov*), and mail the completed form with a filing fee and a nonreturnable recording of the song to the copyright office. The recording doesn't have to be anything fancy—a homemade cassette with a clear vocal and piano or guitar accompaniment will suffice. Who knows whether or not you have a marketable song on your hands, so rather than take the chance on someone else using your work without permission and appropriate compensation, take the time to officially establish proof of authorship.

PRACTICAL GEM
To keep filing fee costs down, you can register several songs under one title (i.e., "Winter Songs, 2004").

Playing Original Song Venues

If you have a finished song that you think is performance-ready, throw it in the mix of your regular repertoire at a gig. It's always interesting and enlightening to just play it without any introduction, and watch how the crowd responds. And if you have several original songs that you'd like to perform, you might want to find an appropriate venue. Coffeehouses and chain bookstores like Borders are usually very receptive to having local singer/songwriters come in for a couple of hours to showcase their original music. From having gone to so many different venues on your field trips, you probably have a good idea of which ones in your area are booking original music versus cover bands. Contact the manager or community relations person of the establishment so you'll know specifically who to address—or better yet, hand deliver your promo package to. The pay for a local original band is traditionally not up to par with that of a cover band, but it's still a great opportunity to try out new songs and get feedback. Furthermore, there's just no denying the joy of singing your own creations.

Living-Room Concerts

Living-room concerts have been around forever, but they have gained popularity in recent years. Traditionally there is a host or patron who sends out invitations for a house party in which an original music

> Songwriting has had an effect on me that I would never have imagined.
> *India.Arie*

performer is entertaining. Snacks and drinks are provided, and there is a minimal cover charge to support the artist. You can propose this arrangement to a devoted fan or family member, or you can come up with a workable variation. Maybe you have acquaintances who would like to hire you to provide live music at a birthday or graduation party in their home. As long as you throw in some cover songs with your originals, you can get performance experience with your new material and add just the right touch to a celebration.

Getting Your Music Heard

There was a time not too long ago when the only ways to get your original music or act heard by people in the music industry were (1) to live in a major music city and go begging door to door, (2) pay big money to an entertainment lawyer to represent you to the record labels, or (3) be fortunate enough to have a personal contact. Thanks to a fee-based service called TAXI (*www.taxi.com*), those days are long gone. TAXI not only has working professionals (songwriters, producers, musicians, etc.) who can help with the songwriting process by critiquing your songs and giving constructive feedback, but they can also help you get your music into the hands of the industry's top decision-makers. I'm talking about music supervisors looking for material to place in TV shows, videos, and movies; music libraries looking for music to supply to businesses of all kinds, as well as publishers and record companies looking for the next big thing. If you're looking to go beyond your local music market for opportunities, I can tell you from firsthand experience that TAXI is your vehicle.

Your Name in Lights

Ask ten famous professional vocal- ists what they did to reach super- stardom, and you'll get ten different stories. There's no one

> Not everyone has heard my name. I want it to be a household name.
> *Mandy Moore*

road to the top, but for those of you who ultimately want to see your name in lights, I think it is safe to say that you'll have to travel to get there. We've all heard the stories of talent being discovered in remote, hole-in-the-wall places by big-time producers who happen to be passing through town. But with few exceptions, the majority of success stories happen because a vocalist did one of two things: She built up a local following and then took her act on the road to build a bigger fan base; this attracted the attention of a major record label. Or, she has moved to (or frequently visited) one of four main loca- tions to be in the middle of the action. These four locations are: Nashville, for country, gospel, and contemporary Christian music; Seattle, for alternative music; and Los Angeles and New York City, for all other forms of pop music.

RESEARCH

I highly recommend that you do your research before deciding on any course of action. Just as you studied and investigated the local music scene in order to make a successful debut, you need to pre- pare in the same way to tackle the national music scene. There are several books that can help you map out a realistic plan by giving you a crash course on how the music industry functions in general. Others are available that target a particular musical genre and give more specific advice.

The service TAXI also holds a yearly three-day seminar for its members, in which it provides workshops, showcases, and question- and-answer sessions with major and independent record-company executives. There are resources out there, and it's your job now to find them. Excuse me for being trite, but knowledge is power, and the reason this saying has become a cliché is because it's true. So empower yourself.

BOOKS TO BEGIN YOUR MUSIC INDUSTRY EDUCATION

❈ *Making It in the Music Business* by Lee Wilson (Allworth Press)
❈ *All You Need to Know about the Music Business* by Donald S. Passman (Simon & Schuster)
❈ *FabJob Guide to Become a Pop Star* by Kathy Baylor (Fabjob.com)
❈ *The Ultimate Survival Guide to the New Music Industry* by Justin Goldberg (Lone Eagle Publishing)

If you choose to seek fame, I must send you on your way to find more experienced teachers in this arena. But there is one last bit of advice I can give you with absolute certainty, no matter which path you choose: Continue with the same love, work ethic, and passion that you've applied to your career thus far, and anything is possible.

Now dazzle, diva!

To Sum It Up

> Just don't give up trying to do what you really want to do. Where there is love and inspiration, I don't think you can go wrong.
> *Ella Fitzgerald*

In this final chapter, I make sure you know what to do to continue your reign as a diva in your local music market, as well as get you ready to take on the world. By adhering to just three simple rules, the possibilities will remain endless, because each rule fuels the others and continues the cycle of excellence. Regularly do a mental checklist or refer back to this chapter to ward off any chance of becoming complacent or stagnant. Continue writing in your diva diary for clues to emerge of a new direction, desire, or dream.

Writing this book, and having it find its way to you, has been my dream. For the diva, the work is never-ending, but it is always a highly rewarding labor of love.

A DIVA NEXT DOOR SAYS

One thing I can say to anyone in the business is to take everything you hear with a grain of salt—both the positives and the negatives. People will tell you that they can make you a star, that they are going to tell their neighbor (who is a major producer) about you, and that you are the best and most beautiful singer they've ever heard. They'll also tell you that they've never heard a worse singer in their life, or ask when the other band is coming back that you are filling in for. They all have their own personal motives for saying what they do, so I've learned not to take the positive feedback too seriously or the negative comments to heart. If someone is really interested in your talent and serious about making a legitimate deal, he'll take a card and call you at home to discuss business. As far as the other negative stuff, everyone has an opinion, but mine of myself is the one I listen to. —Valerie

Sample Thank-You Note

Diva Nextdoor
123 Rising Star Lane
Fabulous, FL 12345
(123) 123-4567

January 5, 2005

Dear Sally,

It was so nice to meet you this weekend when you were performing at the Tasty Restaurant Lounge. I really enjoyed your singing, and I wanted to thank you for taking the time to speak with me on your break. You were very helpful in answering all the questions I had about life as a professional vocalist in our area.

I've joined your mailing list, and I hope to come see you perform again very soon.

Sincerely,

Diva Nextdoor

Sample Cover Letter/Bio

Diva Nextdoor
123 Rising Star Lane
Fabulous, FL 12345
(123) 123-4567

August 1, 2005

The Heartbeat Band
Terry Bandleader
1234 Hireme Street
Rightaway, FL 12344

Dear Terry,

Enclosed please find my demo, photo, and song list in response to your ad in Friday's *Post*. My performance experience includes singing backup for local singer/songwriter Marianne Flemming, and singing blues and jazz standards with the house band at the Artsbar "Jam" every Tuesday night.

As you can see from my song list, I sing a broad variety of styles and welcome the opportunity to expand my repertoire to include all the classic rock songs that your band does so well. After listening to my demo, I hope you'll be inspired to call me so we can arrange an audition in person.

In rock we trust,

Diva Nextdoor

Sample Performance Agreement

Diva Nextdoor
123 Rising Star Lane
Fabulous, FL 12345
(123) 123-4567

Agreement made as of the _____ day of _____, 20____ between the parties identified below. The EMPLOYER listed below agrees to hire the below identified ARTIST to perform, and the ARTIST agrees to provide such performance services under the following terms and conditions:

_____
ARTIST

_____
EMPLOYER

_____
EMPLOYER ADDRESS

_____
EMPLOYER PHONE

_____
PLACE OF PERFORMANCE ADDRESS

_____
DATE OF PERFORMANCE

TIME OF PERFORMANCE / SET LENGTH

LOAD IN / SOUND CHECK TIME

PAYMENT AMOUNT (GUARANTEED)

SOUND SYSTEM PROVIDED BY

ADDITIONAL TERMS

This is intended to be a legally binding contract. In the event of any litigation arising out of this agreement, the prevailing party shall be entitled to reasonable attorney's fees and court costs.

For ARTIST:

AUTHORIZED REPRESENTATIVE SIGNATURE

PRINTED NAME

For EMPLOYER:

AUTHORIZED REPRESENTATIVE SIGNATURE

PRINTED NAME

EMPLOYER agrees to return signed copy and $_____ nonrefundable deposit via regular mail to ARTIST no later than _____ days before performance date.

Sample Wedding Information Sheet

RECEPTION DATE AND TIME

BRIDE'S NAME

GROOM'S NAME

Wedding Party Introduction? ☐ Yes   ☐ No

PARENTS OF THE BRIDE

PARENTS OF THE GROOM

FLOWER GIRL

RING BEARER

BRIDESMAID(S)   (ESCORTED BY) GROOMSMEN

1.

2.

3.

4.

5. _____   _____

6. _____   _____

_____
MAID / MATRON OF HONOR

_____
BEST MAN

_____
BRIDE AND GROOM TO BE ANNOUNCED AS

First Dance? ☐ Yes   ☐ No
_____
SONG REQUEST

Champagne Toast? ☐ Yes   ☐ No
_____
IF YES, BY WHOM?

Garter/Bouquet? ☐ Yes   ☐ No
_____
SONG REQUEST

Cake Cutting? ☐ Yes   ☐ No
_____
SONG REQUEST

Father/Daughter Dance? ☐ Yes   ☐ No
_____
SONG REQUEST

Mother/Son Dance? ☐ Yes   ☐ No
_____
SONG REQUEST

Are there any announcements (birthdays, anniversaries, etc.) you'd like to be announced, or special instructions for the band? ☐ Yes   ☐ No

_____

_____

Recommended Books, Videos, and Web Sites

Diva Biographies

Clooney, Rosemary, and Joan Barthel. *Girl Singer: An Autobiography*. New York: Doubleday, 1999.

Dion, Celine. *Celine Dion: My Story, My Dream*. New York: Avon Books, 2000.

Gray, Scott. *On Her Way: The Shania Twain Story*. New York: Ballantine Books, 1998.

Nassour, Ellis. *Honky Tonk Angel: The Intimate Story of Patsy Cline*. New York: St. Martin's Press, 1993.

Nicholson, Stuart. *Ella Fitzgerald: A Biography of the First Lady of Jazz*. New York: Da Capo Press, 1995.

O'Meally, Robert G. *Lady Day: The Many Faces of Billie Holiday*. New York: Da Capo Press, 2000.

Turner, Tina, and Kurt Loder. *I, Tina*. New York: Avon Books, 1986.

Fashion and Beauty

Aucoin, Kevyn. *Making Faces*. New York: Little, Brown & Co., 1999.

Pierce, Shirley, and Janet Behmer. *Dress Me Now!*. Studio City, CA: Core Concepts, 2000.

Quant, Mary. *Ultimate Makeup & Beauty Book*. New York: Dorling Kindersley Publishing, 1996.

Stover, Laren, and Ruben Toledo. *The Bombshell Manual of Style.*
New York: Hyperion, 2001.
Fred Flare (*www.fredflare.com*), (718) 599-9221
Sephora (*www.sephora.com*), (877) 737-4672

Health and Fitness

Pivonka, Elizabeth, and Barbara Berry. *5 a Day: The Better Health Cookbook: Savor the Flavor of Fruits and Vegetables.* New York: Rodale Books, 2003.
Sinatra, Stephen, M.D. *Optimum Health: A Natural Lifesaving Prescription for Your Body and Mind.* New York: Bantam, 1998.
Shaping Up with Weights for Dummies. Anchor Bay Entertainment, Troy, MI, 2000. (DVD and VHS)
Yoga for Every Body. Bodywisdom Media, Bethesda, MD, 2002. (DVD and VHS)
Tafoy, Carmela, personal trainer (*www.noexcuseworkshops.com*)

Karaoke Resources Online

East Coast Karaoke (*www.eastcoastkaraoke.com*)
Karaoke Bay (*www.karaokebay.com*)
Karaoke Now (*www.karaokenow.com*)
Priddis (*www.priddis.com*)
Shop Karaoke (*www.shopkaraoke.com*)
Singing Machine (*www.singingmachine.com*)

Music Business and Related Subjects

Baylor, Kathy. *FabJob Guide to Become a Pop Star.* Calgary, Alberta, Canada: Fabjob.com Ltd., 2003.

Baker, Bob. *Guerrilla Music Marketing Handbook: 201 Self-Promotion Ideas for Songwriters, Musicians and Bands*. St. Louis: Spotlight Publishing, 2001.

Goldberg, Justin. *The Ultimate Survival Guide to the New Music Industry*. Los Angelas: Lone Eagle Publishing, 2004.

Rusch, Gloria. *The Professional Singer's Handbook*. Milwaukee: Hal Leonard, 1998.

Sward, Diane Rapaport. *How to Make & Sell Your Own Recording*. Englewood Cliffs, NJ: Prentice-Hall, 1999.

Wilson, Lee. *Making It in the Music Business: The Business and Legal Guide for Songwriters and Performers*. 3rd Ed. New York: Allworth Press, 2004.

Broadjam (*www.broadjam.com*)

Chick Singer Night (*www.chicksingernight.com*)

The Diva Next Door (*www.thedivanextdoor.net*)

Gig Finder (*www.gigfinder.com*)

iTunes (*www.apple.com/itunes/store*)

Library of Congress Copyright Office (*www.copyright.gov*)

Real One Rhapsody (*www.Real.com*)

Shavano Music Online (*www.colomar.com/shavano*)

TAXI (*www.taxi.com*)

Songwriting

Braheny, John. *The Craft and Business of Songwriting*. Cincinatti: Writers Digest Books, 2001.

Peterik, Jim, Dave Austin, and Mary Ellen Bickford. *Songwriting for Dummies*. Indianapolis: Wiley Publishing, Inc., 2002.

The Muse's Muse (*www.musesmuse.com*)

The Songwriter's Tip Jar (*www.songwriterstipjar.com*)

Spiritual Guides

Ban Breathnach, Sarah. *Simple Abundance: A Daybook of Comfort and Joy.* New York: Warner Books, 1995.

Cameron, Julia. *The Artist's Way: A Spiritual Path to Higher Creativity.* New York: G.P. Putnam's Sons, 1992.

Werner, Kenny. *Effortless Mastery.* New Albany, IN: Jamey Aebersold Jazz, Inc., 1996.

Wise, Nina. *A Big New Free Happy Unusual Life: Self-Expression and Spiritual Practice for Those Who Have Time for Neither.* New York: Broadway Books, 2002.

Vocal Health and Technique

Allen, Jeffrey. *The Secrets of Singing Female Voice: Low and High Voice with CD.* Miami: Warner Bros. Publications, 2000.

The Singer's Toolbox Featuring Mark Baxter. Milwaukee: Hal Leonard Corporation, 1996. (DVD and VHS)

The Vocalist's Guide to Fitness, Health and Musicianship. Milwaukee: Hal Leonard Corporation, 1991. (DVD and VHS)

Vocal Practice for Performance. Milwaukee: Hal Leonard Corporation, 2003. (DVD and VHS)

The Singing Spot (*www.thesingingspot.com*)

Vocalist (*www.vocalist.org.uk*)

Wake Forest University Center for Voice Disorders (*www.bgsm.edu/voice/medicine_vocal_arts.html*)

Diva Dictionary

a capella: Without instrumental accompaniment

alto: A low female singing voice

ballad: A song slow in tempo that is usually romantic or sentimental in nature

cans: An industry term for headphones

chops: The ability to go from note to note with ease

club date: A gig in which musicians show up unrehearsed and read music charts that the bandleader has provided

continuous: A gig in which the members of the band take breaks one person at a time so that the remaining members of the band can provide music continuously throughout the affair

cover band: A band who covers other artists' material and whose repertoire consists mainly of popular songs

diaphragmatic breathing: Breathing in which the respiratory efforts are done by the abdominal muscles

gig: A job in which a person or group is hired to provide musical entertainment

headshot: A photograph of a person from the neck up

house gig: A work situation in which an establishment hires a band as their premier entertainment to perform at the same times every week

octave: A tone that is eight full tones above or below another given tone

perfect pitch: The ability to identify a musical note on the scale without a single reference

pitch: The relative position of a tone in a scale

repertoire: The stock of songs that a singer is prepared to perform

reverb: A feature on many mixing boards that causes the sound to re-echo

song form: The structure of a particular song (as in the most common form of A-B-A-B-C-B; or verse, chorus, verse, chorus, bridge, chorus)

soprano: The highest natural singing voice found in women and in young boys

steady: See **house gig**

sweet spot: The area of your range in which you are the strongest and most comfortable

tempo: The rate of speed at which music is to be played or a song is to be sung

tone: A sound of distinct pitch, quality, and duration

vibrato: A tremulous or pulsating effect produced in a vocal tone by barely perceptible minute and rapid variations in pitch

work-for-hire: An agreement between an employer and an artist in which the artist is paid a one-time fee for a creative work

Index

Aaliyah, 103
affirmations, 95–96
agents, 140–142. *See also*
   booking
   handing cards for, 141
   negotiating deals with,
      140
   references of, 141–142
Alice, 134
*All You Need to Know
   about the Music
   Business* (Passman),
   181
American Idol, 14, 114
Amos, Tori, 36
Andress, Patricia Cathcart
   (of Tuck and Patty),
   170
Andrews, Jessica, 66
Andrews, Julie, 26, 27
The Andrews Sisters, 17
Aretha's Best, 66
Arie, India, 179
Aucoin, Kevyn, 117
audience
   favorable response of,
      80–81
   myth of, 104
   obnoxious behavior of,
      105, 158–159
   schmoozing, 156
auditions
   being safe, 131
   "domino effect,"
      166–167
   overpreparation for,
      132
   preparation for, 3, 132
   questions for, 130
   top ten mistakes of,
      135
Auld Lang Syne, 162

Baking music, 66
band
   interviewing of, 135
   "mommy bands,"
      49–50
   romances within, 136
   starting of, 173
Barnie, 88
Barrino, Fantasia, 21
Baylor, Kathy, 181
Benatar, Pat, 54, 90
*The Best of Miss Peggy
   Lee*, 66
"better than nothing" day,
   64–65
booking
   by agent, 138–139
   by self, 137–138
books
   recommendations of,
      181, 189–192
Bootylicious, 27
Branch, Michelle, 12
breathing. *See also Happy
   Birthday*
   diaphramatic, 28–30
   evaluation of, 28–29
   to strengthen, 29–30
   while singing, 35
Brightman, Sarah, 30
Broadjam, 50
burnout
   avoiding, 21
   with exercise, 64

Cabaret, 90
caffeine
   dehydration from, 39
Callaway, Ann Hampton,
   170, 172
Cara, Irene, 21
Carey, Mariah, 17, 21, 47

Carlton, Vanessa, 140
Carpenter, Karen, 83
Cher, 47, 95, 112
Chick Singer Night, 94
choices
   goals supported by, 13
Clarkson, Kelly, 4
cleansing ritual, 133
Cline, Patsy, 37, 80, 90
clothes. *See wardrobe*
club dates, 161
colds/coughs. *See also
   remedies*
   prevention of, 39
   singing with, 40
   supplements for, 40–41
Cole, Natalie, 112, 129
Columbus, Christopher,
   170
Colvin, Shawn, 170, 177
Come Rain or Come Shine,
   12
concerts, living room, 179
confidence, 143
contracts, 137–138, 185
Cool Down Smoothie, 72
copyright registration,
   177–178
cover letter/bio, 119, 184.
   See also résumé
Crazy, 80, 90
Crow, Sheryl, 66, 118

Dearie, Blossom, 170
demo
   recording, 19
   for résumé, 120–121
Destiny's Child, 21, 27, 66
diaphramatic breathing
   becoming second
      nature, 30
   exercises for, 29

source of, 28
Dick Tracy, 32
dieting, 65–66
Difranco, Ani, 173
Dion, Celine, 14, 66, 171
diva
  anthems for, 21
  biographies of, 50–51
  breakfast for, 23
  creed for, 24
  diary of, 33
  dictionary for, 193–194
  direct route in becoming, 3–4
  discoveries of, 170
  readiness exercise for, 22–23
  résumé for, 119
  style starters for, 113
"diva biscotti," 67–68
Diva Next Door, 50
diva next door. See testimonials
diva-in-concert videos, 47
diva-in-training, 6–7
The Dixie Chicks, 21, 66
Don't Know Why, 152

Earplugs, 148
East Coast Karaoke, 53
Ekdahl, Lisa, 170
Electric Slide, 80
Electro Voice N/D767, 110
Elliot, Missy, 90
entertainment rag magazines, 51
enunciation, 27
Estefan, Gloria, 43, 91
etiquette, 98–99
Evergreen, 90
Evolution, 66
exercise
  cardio work, 62–63
  creating habit of, 64
  fitness program, 61–63
  motivation to, 60
  for muscle groups, 63
  walking as, 61
  weight training, 62–63
eyebrows
  shaping of, 118

Fabian, Lara, 81
FabJob Guide to Become a Pop Star (Baylor), 181
Falling into You, 66
fame, 180–182
fan base, 102–103, 135–136
fear
  facing of, 27–28
  handicap of, 25–26
  releasing through the prayer, 96
  self doubt, 19
  stage fright, 95, 159
  unfamiliar experiences, 17
Feelings, 131
female greats, 82
female voice, 11
finances
  entertainment business accountant for, 91
  negotiating fees, 137
  overtime/"continuous," 137
  records of, 91
  for self employment, 90–91
first impressions, 133–134
Fitzgerald, Ella, 37, 66, 90, 134, 181
five-a-day bracelet plan, 71–72
Fleming, Renee, 12
FLY, 66
foreign languages, 171
Franklin, Aretha, 3, 21, 37, 66, 90
Fred Flare, 112
Freebird, 141
Freelon, Neena, 170

Garland, Judy, 171
gastric reflux disease, 41
Gaynor, Gloria, 90
Gig Finder, 50
gigs
  attitude towards, 166
  eating and drinking during, 157–158
  lessons from, 155–156
  preparation for, 149
  reneging on, 148–149
  special kinds of, 160–162
  steadiness of, 135–136
Gilberto, Astrid, 90
Girl from Ipanema, 90
The Girlie Show, 47
goals
  choices supporting, 13
  clues to, 56
  obstacles to, 1–2
  reminding by writing, 15
  specifying, 12
Goldberg, Justin, 181
golden rule, 20, 45, 54, 99, 103, 111, 116, 131, 150, 155, 156, 165
Google, 84
Gorme, Eydie, 170
Gray, Macy, 36

Hair, 115–116
Happy Birthday, 30, 35
Happy Girl, 21
Havah Nagilah, 17
headphones, 175
headshot, 119
health. See also colds/coughs
  effect on singing, 73
  food for, 39
  food for, of heart, 23
  insurance for, 91
  for looking good, 73
  psychological effects of, 73
hearing loss, 148
Hill, Faith, 47, 99
Hit Me with Your Best Shot, 90
Holiday, Billie, 36
Horne, Lena, 138
Hot, Hot, Hot, 80
Houston, Whitney, 10
Hynde, Chrissie, 112

I Believe, 21
I Will Survive, 90
I'm a Woman, 21
image, 97
Imbruglia, Natalia, 171

imitation, 26
Indigo Girls, 62, 136
Itsy Bitsy Spider, 25
iTunes, 82

Jackson, Janet, 47
jobs
    getting/keeping, 80
    improving of, 167
    opportunities for, 52
    security of, 103
Jones, Nora, 152
Jones, Ricki Lee, 36
Joplin, Janis, 29
journal notes, 34
junk food, 48

Karaoke Bay, 53
karaoke CD
    choice of, 53–54
    singing with, 86
Karaoke Now, 53
k.d. lang, 50
Kent, Stacey, 170
Knowles, Beyonce, 47, 159
Krall, Diana, 170
Krauss, Alison, 170

LaBelle, Patti, 166
laryngitis, 41
Lavin, Linda, 134
learning
    from masters, 82
    by watching, 45
Lee, Peggy, 21, 66, 141
lighting, 152–153
Live at Wembley, 47
Live in Berlin, 66, 134
Live in Concert, 47
live music
    field trips, 43, 55–57
    to inspire, 46, 169–170
    learning from, 169
    observation of, 44
    occasions for, 17–18
    variables in, 104
    ways to find, 51–52
long tones, 32–33
Lopez, Jennifer, 89, 170
Lucky Beans and Rice, 69
Lullaby of Birdland, 82
Lynn, Loretta, 168
lyrics

finding of, 84
forgetting of, 88, 154
memorizing of, 83–84

Mack the Knife, 134
Madonna, 47, 60, 66, 137
    flawless technique of,
        32
magazines. *See* entertain-
    ment rag magazines
mailing list, 102–103
Make It Happen, 21
make-up, 116–117
    bronzers, 115
    to reflect light, 116
Making Faces (Aucoin), 117
*Making It in the Music Busi-
    ness* (Wilson), 181
Mama's Veggie Beef Soup,
    68–69
manicures, 117
Marcovicci Andrea, 84
McBride, Martina, 21, 66
McEntire, Reba, 87
McGovern, Maureen, 91
McLachlan, Sarah, 92
Messina, Jo Dee, 94
metronome, 84
microphone
    purchase of, 109–110
    technique, 86
Midler, Bette, 26, 64
Minelli, Liza, 35, 37, 90
Monroe, Marilyn, 158
Moore, Mandy, 180
moral support, 142
mouth
    form of, 31–32
MTV Unplugged, 47
Muse's Muse, 177
music
    basic theory classes,
        173
    collection of, 37
    key changes for, 147
    knowledge of, 89–90
    rules for pop, 27
    store, 48–49
Music, 66
music industry
    books about, 181
    marketing to, 179
    researching of, 180–181

My Guy, 90

Name change, 121–122
Nathan, David, 50
naysayers, 18
negativity, 10, 45
nervous energy, 96
networking, 46
New Year's Eve, 161–162
Nicks, Stevie, 36, 112, 113
Night and Day, 90
No Doubt, 66
"The No Excuse Workout,"
    62
Noa, 170
no-coincidences question-
    naire, 56
Now, 66

O'Neli, Jamie, 13
online sources
    for karaoke, 53
    for music community,
        49
    for music stores, 82
Orgill, Roxane, 50–51
Overture Oatmeal, 23

"**P**ackaging" act, 44
Parton, Dolly, 111, 161
passion
    as magic ingredient,
        9–10
Passman, Donald S., 181
Pasta Divine, 70–71
patience, 13, 106
patter, 155
pedicures, 117
percussion
    as education, 83
    for performing,
        110–111
performing
    avoiding "flatness,"
        87–88
    finding opportunities
        for, 93–94
    making contacts by, 17
    mistakes, 134
    rules of conduct,
        153–154
photos
    headshot, 119

photo-op, 156–157
by professionals, 120
pitch
center of, 32–33
in studios, 175
placement
method for, 30
positive attitude, 45
positive reinforcement, 21
practice
daily, 103–104
effect of, 32
maintaining interest in,
46
practice journal, 33–34
practice schedule
creating, 33–34
efficiency for, 34–35
practice space, 34
Prince, Faith, 13
professionalism, 77, 162
progress
making of, 85
understanding of, 15
Proud Mary, 90

Queen Latifah, 160
questionnaires, 10, 22–23,
56, 130

Ray, Amy, 136
Real One Rhapsody, 82
recording
CD, 174
at home, 36
in professional studios,
120–121, 174–176
for résumé, 120–121
for video demo, 169
rehearsals, 145–146
relationships
with audience, 156
with bartenders, 159
basis of, 100
motives of others,
20–21
with other singers,
99–100
problems with, 19–20
with producers,
174–175
respect for others,
97–98

remedies
for colds, 40
for hoarseness, 150
Zicam cold remedy, 40
repertoire, 79–80
reputation, 98
Respect, 21, 90
résumé
assembling of, 122
contents of, 119
demo for, 120–121
self-promotion with,
123
retirement, 91
reverb, 151
reward plan, 21
rhythm
development of, 49
feeling of, 82–83
shaker-type instrument,
49
Rock Steady, 66
Ronstadt, Linda, 171
Ross, Diana, 79

Saliers, Emily, 62
samples
cover letter/bio, 184
performance agree-
ment, 185–186
thank-you note, 54–55,
183
wedding information
sheet, 187–188
Saturday Night Live, 27, 31
schedule plan, 139–140
self-promotion, 100–101
recording for, 120–121,
169
with résumé, 123
Sephora, 117. See also
make-up
set lists, 152
setup and breakdown,
150–151
*The Shaping Up with
Weights for Dum-
mies*, 63
Shop Karaoke, 53
*Shout, Sister, Shout: Ten
Girl Singers Who
Shaped a Century*
(Orgill), 50–51

Showtime Egg Rolls,
132–133
Shure SM58, 110
Simone, Nina, 162
Simpson, Jessica, 97
Sinatra, Frank, 82
singing
back-up, 94–95
in chorus, 26
as controlled yelling, 30
diversifying style of, 16
donations of, 176
evoking emotion for,
87, 134–135
fixing trouble spots,
84–85
with focus, 86
habits, exercise for, 32
handicaps of, 25–26
hitting highest notes,
84–85
jingles, 175–176
movements with, 89
as passion, 9–10
as physical workout, 59
tools of, 49
singing, in public
challenges of, 105
preparing for, 79
requirements of, 7
Singing Machine, 53
Singing Spot, 50
Smith, Keely, 170
smoky environments, 46–47
soloing
with chest voice, 30
with head voice, 26
songbook, 88
songs
for auditions, 131–132
classics, 89
compiling list of, 79–80
mastering, 81
must-learn, 90
original, performing of,
178–180
phrasing, 83
requests for, 80–81
updating repertoire,
167–168
Songwriter's Tip Jar, 177
songwriting, 176–178
Sooner or Later, 32

The Soulful Divas (Nathan), 50
sound check, 151
sound equipment
communicating needs of, 147
Spears, Britney, 89, 100
Springfield, Dusty, 9
Stairway to Heaven, 141
Star Search, 14
Stefani, Gwen, 112
Sting, 82
Stone, Jess, 135
straight notes, 31
Streisand, Barbra, 37, 47, 60, 85, 90, 172
stress/overwork, 40, 61
style. *See also* singing development of, 82
Superstar Smoothie, 48
The Supremes, 17, 90
Survivor, 21, 66

Tafoya, Carmela, 62
TAXI, 179–181
Taylor, James, 82
teaching, 172
tension
releasing of, 96–97
testimonials
being prepared, 107
confidence of singer, 42
grain of salt, 182
listening to heart, 143
pharmacist/singer, 4
respecting band, 124
self esteem through singing, 24
"sound men," 163
staying onstage, 58
value of humility, 92
weight effecting performance, 74
thank you notes, 54–55, 183
There's Got to Be a Morning After, 91

thrift/consignment stores, 113
throat
bleeding, 41
moisture for, 38–39
Timberlake, Justin, 82
Timeless, 47
Titanic, 131
tone deafness, 32
Tuesday Night Music Club, 66
Turner, Tina, 2, 90
Twain, Shania, 91, 167

Ultimate Diva Workout, The, 62
Ultimate Survival Guide to the New Music Industry, The (Goldberg), 181

Vacations, 172–173
Van Dross, Luther, 82
Vaughn, Sarah, 82
The Velvet Rope Tour, 47
The Very Thought of You, 152
VH1 Divas Live, 47
vibrato, 31
videos. *See also* diva-in-concert videos
recommendations of, 189–192
videotaping, 168–169
visualization, 95–96
vocal nodes or polyps, 37–38
vocal styling
consistency of, 27
for pop music, 31
Vocalist, 50
voice. *See also* female voice
amplification for, 148
appreciating qualities of, 26
exercising of, 25
maintaining, 37, 148

problems, 37
protection for, 38
sore or hoarse, 41
spiciness for, 69
uniqueness of, 36
using moderation, 38
weak delivery of, 84
voice coach
rectifying problems with, 85–86
searching for, 37
voice students
recommendations for, 52

Walking, 61
wardrobe, 111–115
accessories for, 118
appropriate, 44
for free, 113–114
theatrical clothes, 111–112
undergarments, 114–115
warm up plan, 34–35
Warren, Diane, 177
We Will Rock You, 30
websites. *See also* online sources
recommendations of, 189–192
resources for, 50
Welsman, Carol, 146, 170
What a Feeling, 21
When the Lights Go Down, 47
Whiting, Margaret, 12
Wide Open Spaces, 21
Widick, Dr. Mark, 41, 148
Wilson, Lee, 181
Wilson, Nancy, 60
The Wizard of Oz, 112
Wonder, Stevie, 82
"work-for-hire," 177

Yearwood, Trisha, 105
You Go Girl Salad, 106–107

Books from Allworth Press

Allworth Press is an imprint of Allworth Communications, Inc. Selected titles are listed below.

Making It in the Music Business: The Business and Legal Guide for Songwriters and Performers, Third Edition
by *Lee Wilson* (paperback, 6 × 9, 256 pages, $19.95)

The Songwriter's and Musician's Guide to Nashville, Third Edition
by *Sherry Bond* (paperback, 6 × 9, 256 pages, $19.95)

Rock Star 101: A Rock Star's Guide to Survival and Success in the Music Business
by *Marc Ferrari* (paperback, 5½ × 8½ , 176 pages, $14.95)

Gigging: A Practical Guide for Musicians
by *Patricia Shih* (paperback, 6 × 9, 256 pages, $19.95)

Creative Careers in Music, Second Edition
by *Josquin des Pres and Mark Landsman* (paperback, 6 × 9, 240 pages, $19.95)

Career Solutions for Creative People: How to Balance Artistic Goals with Career Security
by *Dr. Ronda Ormont* (paperback, 6 × 9, 320 pages, $19.95)

The Quotable Musician: From Bach to Tupac
by *Sheila E. Anderson* (hardcover, 7¾ × 7¾ , 224 pages, $19.95)

The Secrets of Songwriting: Leading Songwriters Reveal How to Find Inspiration and Success
by *Susan Tucker* (paperback, 6 × 9, 256 pages, $19.95)

The Art of Writing Great Lyrics
by *Pamela Phillips Oland* (paperback, 6 × 9, 272 pages, $18.95)

How to Pitch and Promote Your Songs, Third Edition
by *Fred Koller* (paperback, 6 × 9, 208 pages, $19.95)

Please write to request our free catalog. To order by credit card, call 1-800-491-2808 or send a check or money order to Allworth Press, 10 East 23rd Street, Suite 510, New York, NY 10010. Include $5 for shipping and handling for the first book ordered and $1 for each additional book. Ten dollars plus $1 for each additional book if ordering from Canada. New York State residents must add sales tax.

To see our complete catalog on the World Wide Web, or to order online, you can find us at ***www.allworth.com***.